NO ONE TAKES MY CHILDREN

The Dramatic Story of a Mother's Determination
to Regain her Kidnapped Son and Daughter

Donya al-Nahi
with Eugene Costello

MAINSTREAM
PUBLISHING
EDINBURGH AND LONDON

First published in Great Britain in 2005 by
MAINSTREAM PUBLISHING COMPANY
(EDINBURGH) LTD
7 Albany Street
Edinburgh EH1 3UG

ISBN 1 84018 963 0

In the interests of confidentiality, some names
have been replaced with a pseudonym

Typeset in Baskerville Book

Printed in Great Britain by
Antony Rowe Ltd, Chippenham, Wiltshire

To my sister Tracey, for your love and strength. Even when you had problems of your own, you still gave me time. I love you.

To Marlon and Khalid for never giving up hope, even when things got so bad. What amazing children.

Also to my parents who have made me realise that everyone makes mistakes. I will always love you, whatever has happened in the past. You only have one mother.

And, finally, to those children who are parted from their mothers. Never give up hope that you'll find your mother right next to you, not just in your dreams. And you never know, I might just be with her!

If a bird loved a fish, where would they live?

Contents

Author's Note

The following book is an account of my life and the events that led to the most terrible thing that ever happened to me – my children being abducted by the man I loved and trusted as my husband. This was especially devastating as, up to that point, I had devoted my life to helping mothers who had experienced the same thing. Through all my work helping such women, my husband had always been my rock, supporting me in what I did. I never dreamed for one second that the horrific reality of child abduction could ever befall me.

For this reason, I felt it was important to put this story into the context of my life, to illustrate the events that led to that terrible day. As a result, some of the material recounted in the first chapters of this book was included in *Heroine of the Desert*, my first book. I know that not everyone who reads *No One Takes My Children* will have read it, however some accounts are told there in greater detail and that book contains more stories not told in this one. For those wishing to learn more about my work prior to my own children being taken, I do hope you will read my first book.

And the chief purpose of telling everyone about my work before my own children were taken is a simple one. If it could happen to me – when I had dealt with dozens of such cases and knew what signs to watch out for, to be on guard against – then surely it could happen to any mother in a mixed marriage. That, for me, is the most sobering thought of all.

Donya al-Nahi,
London, March 2005

Prologue

I yanked open the passenger door. Strangely, it was as though the rage had left me. Now I was calm and felt completely in control of the situation. Everything I had been doing for the previous eight weeks had led to this point and now that it was upon me, it was as though something greater than me was guiding my actions, that nothing could stop me now. I reached in and picked up my little girl, Amira, pulling her away from my husband, Mahmoud. The look on his face was one of total shock. He had clearly not believed that I would track them down. Numb, he let me take her without any resistance. Then I pulled open the rear door, allowing my baby son, Allawi, to jump out, his face lighting up, calling out, 'Mummy! Mummy!'

I pulled the two kids towards me and stood there in front of Mahmoud's friend Ali's house in war-torn Baghdad, thousands of miles from home. My older sons, Khalid and Marlon, moved closer to me and grabbed their little brother and sister, kissing and hugging them. Over the tops of their heads I looked at Mahmoud and he held my gaze defiantly. I began to feel nervous for the first time. What would happen now? Who would make the first move? Was Mahmoud simply going to stand by while I took his children

– our children – away, back to England, possibly for him to never see them again? Somehow, I didn't think so.

At that moment, as we all stood rooted to the spot, my sister Tracey suddenly appeared, running up the road towards us. 'Don't worry, Donya,' she shouted across to me. 'I found a squad of American soldiers and explained the situation to them. They're going to take over now.'

I became aware of a low, rumbling noise, the sound of machinery and gears grinding. I looked up the road and saw two enormous tanks turning the corner, heading towards us. It was unbelievable, just like something out of a film. As they moved closer, no one spoke. The two tanks finally pulled up outside the house. There were several American soldiers standing on the tanks in full uniform with helmets, holding guns and looking at us. One of them jumped down. In the dark, it was hard to tell how old he was; he could have been anything from his early 20s to his mid-30s. I suppose he must have been in charge as he seemed to be taking control of the situation.

He turned to me and very respectfully said, 'Good evening, Ma'am. Are you the mother of these children?'

I replied that I was and told him how we had ended up in this mess. The soldier listened intently as I spoke. I finished by saying, 'Now, all I want to do is take my children home, put this awful episode behind us and start to rebuild our lives.'

'OK, Ma'am, we can make that happen for you,' the soldier said.

I could have thrown my arms around him. People often criticise the Americans for their gung-ho attitude, but I had every reason to be thankful for their can-do, let's-make-this-thing-happen approach to problem-solving. It meant I was going to be able to turn around and take my children back where they belonged, away from this war zone – and now, it seemed, nothing could stand in my way. The finishing post was in sight.

Mahmoud took hold of Marlon, begging him to stay that night. It was as though he knew that if he let his children go now, he would never see them again. The soldier intervened, pointing his gun in Mahmoud's direction. He was very polite, but there was the unspoken threat that if Mahmoud did not do as he said, he would be forced to take action.

'You need to back off from the kid, now, Sir,' he said quietly.

'Why do I have to back off?' Mahmoud replied agitatedly. 'These are my children too.'

The soldier stayed calm and said, 'You need to back off now, Sir, because if you do not, I will be forced to arrest you. If you resist arrest, I will be forced to shoot you. Either way, it's going to make all of our lives a whole lot easier if you just do what I tell you and back off now. That's the way it works.'

At that moment, part of me wanted to crumple and cry. How had it come to this? I had a gun in my handbag, there were two tanks in the street and a soldier was threatening my husband at gunpoint. Then I stiffened my resolve. It was Mahmoud who had put us in this situation. I would do whatever I had to do.

Chapter 1

From Small Beginnings . . .

I was born Donna Topen in 1965, but I am now known by my Muslim name, Donya al-Nahi. The press and others have called me, variously, a professional child-snatcher, a kidnapper, the Scarlet Pimpernel and Jane Bond in a headscarf. I prefer to think of myself as a mother first, a friend to other mothers second, then, and only in extreme cases, a child-rescuer third.

I was born in Walton-on-Thames in Surrey to Sandy and Anne Topen. My father was a bear of a man who worked as a flight engineer, while my mother was an attractive and vivacious woman with long, dark hair, who, like so many women of the time, was a housewife. An intelligent and sparkling woman, I often think that if she had been more fulfilled in her life, she wouldn't have been such a difficult and unhappy person.

A journalist once said rather snootily of me and my work that my 'role as maternal avenger feeds some complicated private psychological need'. No doubt he thought he was being especially clever, but the simple truth is that I have always been quite clear that my unhappy childhood and fractious relationship with my mother are what lie behind my unshakeable belief that children have a right to happiness and should always be given the opportunity to be with their mother. I don't see anything wrong with that and I am proud of what I have done to help reunite family members who have been forced to live apart.

My parents were Scottish, from Dundee originally, but moved around a lot due to the nature of my dad's work. The aeronautic industry is a specialised one, so we went wherever my dad's job took him. Perhaps constantly being uprooted, never settling for more than a few years at a time, created an insecurity in me that I do not wish my own children to experience.

My parents did not have what you could call a happy marriage. There was a lot of arguing and many fights. I was born roughly one year before Tracey, my younger sister, and about a year after Sandra; squeezed in between them. Sandra and I are not particularly close, though I have a better relationship with Tracey. As a child, I was the quietest of the three and liked to closet myself away from the shouting and bad feeling by hiding away in my room, playing with my toys. I was different to my sisters, in that they were quite boisterous and played noisily. I always liked to keep my dolls in the boxes in which they came, taking them out every so often to look at them, then packing them away perfectly, keeping them in shop condition. I'm sure a psychologist would say it displayed a compulsive need for order among the chaos and unhappiness. I just thought they looked better that way.

My favourite toy, which became my constant companion, was a hand-knitted pink pig whom I called Percy. He slept with me and helped me keep those naughty dollies in line. One day, I went into my bedroom and found that Sandra and Tracey had hung him by the neck from the light-fitting. I screamed and cried, and was inconsolable even after Dad cut him down and showed me that he was still fine.

As the years passed, the arguments between my parents grew worse and worse, while my relationship with my mother never really developed. Although it will pain her to read this, my memories of her are not warm ones and I recall being smacked by her on many occasions. We are closer now as adults, to an extent, but the pain of an unhappy childhood never really leaves you.

Mum was the disciplinarian of the home. She insisted that we did all our chores: polished our shoes, kept our rooms tidy. On the occasions when we failed to live up to her exacting standards, we would be punished. Added to this was the fact that we seemed to move house quite often, meaning I didn't have close childhood friends. All in all, it made for a cold and forbidding atmosphere at home. When I was about seven, for reasons I couldn't really fathom at the time, my mother left home for a year and Dad was left to look after us. He did his best, of course, but with him working, it was very hard for him. Social workers intervened, and we were looked after while he was at work. After about a year, my mother came home and things returned to their normal, unhappy routine.

My mother seemed to have a lot of Arabic friends. I don't know how she met them or who they were, but somehow I seem to have inherited her affinity for the Middle East and all things Arabic.

There were some happy times, though. I remember, between the ages of nine and twelve, living in a big house in Earith, near St Ives in Cambridgeshire, not far from Soham, which will now always be associated with the awful and brutal murders of those two poor little angels Jessica Chapman and Holly Wells. No one could ever forget that haunting photo of them in their Manchester United shirts taken at a family barbecue, smiling with happiness, their whole lives ahead of them, the day they were murdered. We lived in an enormous Victorian house with servants' quarters and more bedrooms than I can remember. There was also a vast garden, in which my eccentric dad was attempting to build his own aeroplane. These days, he rather wisely sticks to motorbikes.

Back then, I was at the Ramsey Abbey School in Huntingdon, a few miles away, where I made two very good friends, Sarah and Sharon. Sarah, whose nickname was Minkie, was a very pretty little girl who loved horses and showjumping. And Sharon, or

Gertrude as we called her, was very down-to-earth. My nickname was Dodo. I loved both girls dearly. They were my best and only friends.

Unfortunately, this brief interlude of tranquillity was not to last. We soon moved once again, this time to Bushey, a commuter town in Hertfordshire, not far from Watford, and I hated it there. I attended Watford Grammar School, but by now my behaviour was becoming increasingly erratic. I was constantly getting into trouble, being suspended or given detention. I seemed to have a problem with authority, like so many children with unhappy home lives. It seems so self-evident that these problems are caused in the home and this is what has made me so determined that children should not have the consequences of their parents' unhappiness inflicted upon them. That is why, these days, I firmly believe it is better for warring parents to divorce than force their children to endure a miserable upbringing.

The one ray of sunshine at school was my English teacher, John Hilley. I thought he was the bee's knees, as they say. To be quite truthful, I think I had a schoolgirl crush on him. Only he seemed to understand me; he could see the difficulties I was having and how I was being affected by life at home.

I fondly remember going to Spain with my dad when I was about 14. He had to collect a DC-3 for some reason for work and then fly it back to the UK. I was almost sick with excitement when he said I could go with him.

We stayed in a hotel in Spain and one night after dinner, when my dad went to his room, I sneaked down to the bar and met a group of air hostesses, as they used to be called, who were going out clubbing. I looked older than I was, particularly as I was wearing make-up, and so I went with them. When I arrived back at four or five o'clock in the morning, it was already growing light and, to my horror, I could see my dad on the balcony of his room, scanning the area, obviously looking for me. The hotel had its own maze in the gardens, so I crept in there, trying to hide from his gaze. Of course, from the height of his balcony, he could still see me anyway.

'Donna!' he roared. 'What the bloody hell are you doing in that maze? Get up here now before I kill you . . .'

On our way back to the UK, he persuaded the pilot to let me take the controls. We were flying low along the coast of France, looking over the sea, and below us it was a beautiful day with plenty of yachts out sailing. I edged into the seat and tried to listen to the instructions I was being given. When I took the joystick, though, I pulled to one side, and the plane gave a lurch and it dipped. The pilot naturally snatched the controls back, but as I looked out of the window, I noticed that one of the yachts was struggling to stay upright in the slipstream I had inadvertently caused. Being a typical teenager, I found this hilariously funny. Of course, Dad – and the rest of the crew – didn't.

Then, as we flew over France, another thing happened which has stuck in my mind. We had been given a load of frozen chickens to bring home with us by one of Dad's business contacts in Spain. Lovely idea, but by that stage they were completely defrosted and beginning to stink. So we had to fly low enough to open the cockpit hatch and start lobbing them out one by one. Again, this seemed hilarious to me. It was like a low-budget Ealing-comedy version of *The Dam Busters*. Naturally, Dad found these incidents less amusing. He never asked me to accompany him on a work outing again.

By the age of 15, I was so fed up with life at home that I decided I'd had enough. I had no qualms about leaving home, or school. Much as feminist friends would hate to hear it, I had absolutely no desire to go to college, to educate myself and to have a career. All I ever wanted was to have children and become a mum. I wasn't even particularly interested in men – they would just have to be a means to an end, I decided. I got myself a job at a café on Watford High Street working as a waitress and found myself a bedsit in a house on Cassio Road, a busy, soulless thoroughfare near the town centre. The rent was £17.50 a week, and the landlord wanted two weeks' rent upfront. I could manage one week from my first pay packet, but I didn't know where I would find the second. Luckily, Sandra had a gallant Italian boyfriend called Claudio who came to my rescue by lending me the rest. Adulthood had begun.

Chapter 2

She's Leaving Home

I can't pretend that there was anything particularly glamorous about my life during the year which followed. The bedsit was pretty grim, although it was cheap. There was no central heating, so my breath would mist in the mornings and I'd stay in bed until the last possible moment, then leap out like a scalded cat and try to beat my previous record for getting dressed in the shortest possible time. I'll always remember trying to warm my sheets before getting into bed by running a hairdryer up and down the bed. There was an electricity meter in the room, which took 50p pieces and running out was a regular, and unpleasant, experience. But at least I was independent. I was earning enough money from my job in the café to pay my rent and have a modest social life, so I was happy.

It was around this time that I met Karim. He was a Jordanian who was doing a course in business studies at Watford University, and he swept me off my feet. With his olive skin and lustrous brown eyes, he seemed so glamorous and exotic – I really had inherited my mother's fascination with the Middle East. We began seeing each other in earnest and, about a year later, he suggested that I go to Jordan with him to live. Why not, I told myself. There was nothing tying me to Watford – working in a café and living in a poky bedsit was all too easy to give up.

I'm not sure what I was expecting from Jordan, but I suppose I had visions of miles of desert and sand. I was pleasantly surprised. Karim's family lived in a tiny hamlet in the middle of mile after mile of lush green farmland. It was an eye-opener, as was his family's way of life, which seemed to me to have changed little through the centuries.

His parents lived in the main family home within the small community, built in a Jordanian style around an enclosed courtyard so that there was always shade from the sometimes oppressive heat. As far as I could see, all the smaller houses nearby were owned by members of the extended family, with the big house being used for socialising and eating together en masse. For someone with fresh memories of an unhappy, fractured childhood, it seemed truly magical, exuding a warmth and love that I had never experienced. This lifestyle seemed so attractive to me that I wondered why all families didn't live this way.

It seemed to me that this closeness was in part due to their Muslim faith, since great emphasis is placed on the importance of family as a basic building block within the culture. With so many unhappy families back in the UK victims of divorce and separation, it seemed little wonder to me that Jordanian society, or at least the fragment to which I was exposed, was so much more stable. I began to take an interest in the teachings of the Koran and, during my time in Jordan, converted to Islam.

I spent a most wonderful and happy year with Karim's family. It developed in such a way that it seemed everyone expected the next step for Karim and me would be marriage. It was clear that this was his hope and expectation too, and for a while I allowed myself to be seduced by the idea of living in this tranquil and happy society.

But then I realised that I was just too young to be considering getting married – I was only just 17, after all. I had had a taste of freedom and found it hugely to my liking. Was I really prepared to settle down in a tiny community and learn to become a dutiful, housebound Muslim wife at this age? Motherhood, though still my ambition, would have to wait a while. I felt that there was a whole world to be explored, experiences to be had. I tried to communicate my fears to Karim, who was patient and understanding, but seemed to think these nerves would pass. I couldn't seem to make him see that this was the real me: a young girl with an appetite for adventure.

Eventually, I despaired of making him see my point of view. There was only one thing for it. With a heavy heart, I decided it was time to put an end to my rural idyll and return to the 'real world'. I couldn't face telling these lovely people that I was turning my back on them, so I pretended I was simply returning to the UK for a short trip to see my family and would be coming back. I said goodbye to them for the last time and flew home. It wouldn't be the first time I would respond to a difficult situation by running away. In later years, as I came across men who did exactly the same thing to their partners and children, it gave me some insight into their desperation. The cruel punishment that they inflicted on their families was not one I would be prepared to stand idly by and tolerate.

Back in the UK, I spoke to Karim on the phone and tried to make him understand why it had been necessary for me to leave. He felt that it was just a question of giving me time and space, and couldn't understand that I wasn't anywhere near being ready to settle down. It wasn't that I needed a few weeks, even a few months; I had a whole life to live and couldn't ask him to wait for several years while I experienced the world. Reluctantly, he accepted that we were not meant to be together, and we let the relationship go. But I will never forget the love and kindness Karim and his family showed me, nor the fact that it was their simple way of life that turned me to Islam, and sent me further along the road I have taken in life.

It was a curious fact that after leaving home, my relationship with my mother improved. Not dramatically – we have never become close or intimate; there is too much water under the bridge – but the coldness, even dislike, that was evident throughout my childhood thawed a little and we ended up with a cessation of hostilities, an *entente cordiale* between warring factions. I could never feel the warmth towards her that many children feel towards their mothers, and she in return could never display the nurturing care that I always secretly craved. I would describe the relationship between us as more akin to that between distant sisters.

Not long after I'd returned to England following my year in Jordan, we agreed to take a holiday to Tunisia together. While we were out there, like many a young girl before and after me, I had a whirlwind holiday romance. The boy's name was Ahmed, and even now I am not sure what it was that attracted me to him. He was certainly no oil painting, unlike poor handsome Karim.

He was only a year or so older than me – still a kid – and for whatever reason, we had a fling. Ahmed was from wealthy stock: his father was from Qatar and his mother from an affluent Tunisian farming family. He drove a sleek, expensive German car of some description, and my mother was naturally impressed by this superficial display of wealth. She had never approved of Karim with his simple background, so encouraged me in this relationship. Before we were due to head home, out of the blue Ahmed asked me to marry him.

There I was, just a kid, hugely on the rebound. What my mother should have done was to say, 'Don't be so ridiculous, you're far too young for this nonsense.' But, instead, she got as excited as if it was she who had received the proposal. In my confusion, I went along with things and soon found myself being swept along in a torrent of arrangements. My mother sent for an over-the-top white wedding dress, which arrived with Tracey from England. Ahmed's family seemed just as happy with the plan. Perhaps having a pretty young English girl for a daughter-in-law would be prestigious. It was almost as though I was a helpless bystander watching things unfold, while inside I was screaming in horror at the pace of events.

It is the Tunisian custom to throw a lavish pre-wedding party, as extravagant as weddings themselves in the UK, and after which the ceremony itself takes place.

I walked into a huge room packed with guests, some of whom had flown there from the UK and elsewhere. It was as though I was in a dream. All around me, strangers were pressing my arm, murmuring their compliments on my appearance. I looked around for Mum and Tracey, but couldn't see them anywhere. My head was spinning. Across the room, through the assembled guests, I could see the door open and Ahmed enter. He looked so young and so pathetic that I knew in an instant I could not marry him. Without fully realising what I was doing, I got to my feet and began to make my way towards the door, stopping every couple of yards to accept more blessings from well-wishers. Soon, I'd reached the door. I took a deep breath and stepped outside. I knew I would never be going back. In full wedding regalia, I managed to hail a taxi and instructed him to take me to a hotel in the next town.

I waited for a few hours in my room, then rang my mother at her hotel. Far from the attack I had been expecting, she was thoroughly understanding and supportive. She soothed me, and when I explained that my passport was still at Ahmed's house, she became instantly pragmatic. She told me not to worry, that she had some Palestinian friends in Tunis who would be able to sort out another passport for me. I was amazed. I knew she had Arabic friends, but to be able to come up with a plan like that in a foreign country without any drama made me see a side to her I never knew existed. In later years, I found I was also able to stay calm in all kinds of dangerous situations, so perhaps I have inherited my mother's steely resolve.

The following day, some men of slightly dubious appearance came to the hotel and Mum did the talking. Within hours, I had a new passport. We flew home a few days later and, to this day, I have never heard from poor Ahmed again. I only hope that he found a more suitable wife than I could ever have been.

But I wasn't done with my erratic, some would say mad and destructive, behaviour. Back in the UK, a chance meeting at a petrol station with a wealthy Saudi called Mohammed soon led to an affair. I was beginning to think I must have had some hidden signal that attracted only men of Arab descent, a little like the high-pitched whistle that only dogs can hear. I didn't care, though. I was young with no ties, and I intended to have some fun.

Mohammed was very wealthy – he owned a penthouse apartment in London's exclusive Mayfair district – and he treated me well. Money was no object. I was back living with my mother at her house in Bushey – my parents had finally seen the light and divorced. Of course, we were fighting the whole time and one night I started to complain to him about how difficult things were. He seemed puzzled and asked me why I didn't simply move out. 'Fat chance,' I laughed. 'I've hardly got two pennies to rub together.'

The idea of not being able to do something for financial reasons was an alien concept to him, and he threw money at the problem, buying me my own house in Bushey. He was something of a sugar daddy to me. We often went on shopping sprees in London's West End, where he would buy me expensive jewellery and charge it to his American Express account.

He told me that his family back in Saudi were keen for him to marry a cousin of his some 15 years older than him, but that he had no intention of doing so. In fact, he went on to say, he was planning to take me home to meet them. I wasn't sure that I wanted to marry him, despite the life of luxury I would surely be marrying into, but I was flattered nonetheless. But the trip never happened. One day, he told me that he had received bad news from home. His mother had had a heart attack and he had to fly home that day to see her and take care of business. Under the circumstances, this was not the right time to be introduced to his family.

I pretended to sulk, so he softened the blow by telling me that I could charge things to his American Express account while he was away. I took him at his word. At first, I acted with restraint, but as the days became weeks without any sign of him returning, I became like a woman possessed. I was buying jewellery, expensive silverware, anything I could think of. Then I discovered that there were some unscrupulous shop owners who would give me large sums of cash against the account, as long as I signed for a higher amount of goods, so they too could profit from the scam. I was completely out of control.

Then, one day there was a knock on the door. It was two men from American Express. I was petrified, but I managed to keep my head. I insisted that he was my husband, and that I was authorised to use the account. As they only had his Mayfair number and couldn't contact him in Saudi Arabia, they had no choice but to accept my word. You might have thought that would have served as a warning, but I just carried on as before.

Once again, I got a visit from another two faceless men in suits telling me I would have to attend a meeting with the head of security at American Express at an office in central London. I had no choice but to go. My head was spinning, I was in a terrible state. I had literally no idea how much I had spent. I had taken thousands from this account. One canteen of silver cutlery alone had cost £45,000. It had been like an illness; I had been buying things I neither wanted nor needed. The day of reckoning was upon me. I would be in even greater trouble if I didn't attend because the police would surely be called in, I reasoned, and I could find myself in the dock on charges of theft, fraud or obtaining goods by deception. My God, I thought, I could go to prison.

I dressed up as smartly as I could and made my way to the appointment. I was shown into a room and sat down. The head of security came in and made no attempt at small talk. In front of him were papers, statements, times and dates of transactions . . . it was all there in black and white, and I could not talk my way out of this one. I decided to tell the truth, or as near to the truth as I could, and told him that I had been led to understand that this man was going to marry me, but then he suddenly disappeared off to Saudi Arabia, giving me authority to use his charge card, which was true. I said I had grown depressed and turned to binge shopping to comfort myself, a kind of retail bulimia. I was in tears, and I wasn't putting on an act.

He listened to me and said, 'Right, it stops here. Hand back the charge card, don't make any more purchases and we will not press charges. And if you've made a note of the number anywhere else, don't even think about using it. This is your only warning.' I fished the card out of my handbag, handed it to him and he got up and left the room.

That evening, I rang my unknowing benefactor.

'Listen,' I said. 'I've got into a bit of a mess with your American Express card.'

He laughed. 'That doesn't matter. How much are we talking about?'

I gulped and said, 'I believe it's around £750,000.'

There was a long silence and he put the phone down. I never heard from him again – but at least the police hadn't been called in. I'd had another narrow escape.

Chapter 3

Learning to Fly

After this close call, I sold the house in Bushey and moved down to Maida Vale in north-west London. I rented an apartment in a block of mansion flats and life was fine. I was young, I had no ties and, due to my escapades, I had a degree of financial independence. One of my indulgences was taking holidays to sunnier climes when I could and, late in 1989, when I was 24 and still had my looks, I went to Cyprus for a break and a bit of winter sun. My man-magnet was still working, or so it seemed – I met a lovely man named Theo, who fell for me. We came across one another in a hotel on the first day of my holiday and were soon enjoying a full-blown holiday romance. He was kind and considerate, and wealthy too, with a half-Cypriot, half-Saudi heritage. A pattern was definitely beginning to emerge, I thought to myself with a wry smile. It wasn't that I was attracted to men with money – certainly not when I think about the second man I chose to marry, Mahmoud, a man of modest means who worked as a waiter – it was just that they seemed to be attracted to me.

It was a lovely little holiday fling, and it didn't hurt anybody. I even met his mother, a stocky, down-to-earth Cypriot named Flora, whom I liked instantly. But when the holiday drew to an end, as holidays must, I thought the romance would too. I hadn't banked on Theo and his persistence. Back in London, I would receive daily phone calls from him telling me how much he missed me and asking when I was coming back out. We spoke over the weeks that followed and I went back out to see him a few times. It was clear that *he* had decided I was marriage material, but I wasn't so sure. With all my close escapes, I really wanted to be sure before I committed to one man. I saw myself as the sort of girl who, if I was going to marry, wanted to do it properly.

The issue was forced, though, when I went to visit him in the summer of 1990 and became pregnant. Theo was delighted, and so was I, to be honest. I said earlier that all I had ever wanted was to become a mother, and now it was happening. There was absolutely no question of not having the baby, a choice many women in Britain might have made. For one thing, Islam does not allow it – strictly speaking, this even applies in cases of rape, since every life is sacred – and I was now a practising Muslim. But more importantly, I wanted this child. I felt whole and fulfilled and content. The idea of living on that peaceful island, with a kind and generous husband and year-round sun, seemed like heaven.

We were to have a civil wedding in Paphos, one of the island's main towns. My mother came over for the ceremony, but didn't endear herself to her future in-laws by seeming to pick up a bevy of young Arabic men and staying out late every night clubbing. After the wedding, when she had gone back home, I started to panic. There was little for me to do on the island, although all my material needs were catered for handsomely – I even had a Sri Lankan maid named Anna to keep me company. But, inside, I was beginning to go out of my mind.

I didn't know anyone and spent the whole day with Anna while Theo was out working. There was nothing for me to do and, despite the beauty of the island, I felt trapped; a prison with beautiful gardens is still a prison. I started to go to pieces. I was trapped once again. True to form, my thoughts turned to escape. My belly was growing each day with the child inside me, and if I didn't make my move soon, I would be prevented from flying; I would be over the safe period of seven months, after which you are not supposed to fly. And it would be so much harder to leave with a newborn baby. I had to act.

I took Anna into my confidence. I told her she could come to the UK with me, but she would have to help me get away. It would all have to be planned meticulously. I arranged for a removal company to come whilst Theo was at work on the day that we were to make our move; there would be just enough time for them to pack up my belongings and take them away to be shipped to England later. Then we would have to head straight to the airport to catch an afternoon flight back to the UK before Theo realised what had happened. I suppressed my feelings of guilt at what I was doing. There would be plenty of time for that later.

We got to the airport and onto a flight. As the plane took off, I looked down on this island that could have been my home. It looked alien and remote, like the holiday destination it was to me, not the place I was to spend the rest of my life.

Going back to London felt like the natural choice. I still had my flat in Maida Vale, thank God, and Anna came to stay with me there. Theo rang, of course, but the outburst of rage that I had been expecting never came. He was patient and sensitive, saying that he could understand my fears. But he also pointed out that I had probably panicked without giving things a chance. One by one, he took my arguments and overcame them. My loneliness, he said, was only to be expected, but I wasn't the only British mother on the island – why, there was a large English expat community with whom I could socialise and make friends. And once our child started school, I would meet other mothers. His arguments were all the more convincing for being so gently delivered.

Some weeks later, I gave birth to my first child, a beautiful baby boy with black hair and deep dark eyes. I named him Marlon. Over the next few months, Theo continued to ring and persuaded me to go back with Marlon for a visit. He was so forgiving and happy to see his son that I felt confused again. Each time I visited, he put no pressure on me to stay and didn't make a scene when I said I was returning to the UK. He accepted everything with the quiet dignity that he had always shown. Gradually, the trips became longer and the visits back to London less frequent. When Marlon was three, I agreed to allow him to be enrolled in a nursery school on the island. I was once again slipping into accepting the status quo.

Then suddenly all my doubts returned. I saw the years slipping away from me, my life chained to this rock in the Mediterranean, as the bonds we'd made grew only stronger. My son would learn Greek, and I would be forced to live out my years unfulfilled and lonely. I would become like one of the women in the villages around me, concerned only with putting a good meal on the table. I couldn't face it, and if that is selfish of me, so be it.

For a second time, I planned our escape. Once again, Anna was to come back to London. I bought the flights and booked a taxi to the airport; we stopped off at the school to explain that Marlon had a doctor's appointment, and took him into the taxi with us. That evening we were back in the flat in Maida Vale. This time, though, Theo did not take it with good grace. He came on the next available flight and turned up at the flat. He was livid, enraged, shouting at me that I was the most cruel and selfish person that he had ever met. I can't say that I blamed him. I would have felt exactly the same.

When he saw Marlon, his rage turned into sadness. He held Marlon and sobbed. Eventually, he looked up at me. 'Donya,' he said, 'I cannot force you to do something against your will, but you must understand that I have not only lost a wife, I have also lost a son.' For any man, that is difficult; for an Arabic man, even more so.

In the years that lay ahead of me, I would often think of Theo when I was helping a mother to rescue her child. He gave me an insight and an understanding into the way such men think. I, too, had done the same, being unable or unwilling to live in another culture. It meant that I would never condemn a man out of hand for what he had done – I knew only too well the desperation and fear that leads to such a dramatic course of action. But, except in the rarest of cases, I would always stand by my firm belief that a child should not be parted from its mother. The best solution is always to ensure that both parents are involved in the child's upbringing, and, for that reason, I never sought to prevent Theo access to his son. He learned to accept the situation and has remained a good friend. We still speak on the phone to this day.

By now, it was the summer of 1994 and I was 29. My childhood ambition of becoming a mother had been realised, though it wasn't quite in the manner I'd envisaged in my girlish daydreams. Anna, Marlon and I were sharing my flat in Maida Vale and, despite the traumas I had been through – many self-inflicted, admittedly – it wasn't a bad life.

One Saturday around this time, Tracey came to visit me and we decided we'd order a takeaway from Maroush, a Lebanese restaurant I knew on London's Edgware Road, or Little Beirut, as some call it, thanks to all the Middle Eastern restaurants there, and the coffee shops where old men sit puffing away on their hookahs night and day. We ordered my favourite dish, one that I have always loved, called bamya, which is made from okra, and my friend went to collect it. We were starving and I couldn't wait to tuck in. When we opened the containers in the kitchen, though, we discovered they had given us the wrong things.

I got straight on the phone to them, but the guy who took the call didn't seem to be taking me all that seriously. I got cross and demanded to speak to the manager. When he came on, I told him in my firmest no-nonsense voice that they had given us the wrong order and, as it was their mistake, they had better send someone round to sort it out. I gave him the address, then put the phone down. Sure enough, 20 minutes later, the doorbell rang. It was the guy to whom I had first spoken.

'I had to meet the lady I spoke to on the phone in person,' he said with a smile.

I was in no mood for his foolish nonsense, so I told him to take the food through to the kitchen. I have to admit, though, he was attractive in a roguish kind of way: he was of slim build with mischievous eyes and a cheeky, lopsided grin. I thanked him and sent him away.

The next night, feeling lazy, we decided to order in again. Maroush don't do deliveries, or they didn't then, so the guy taking the order told me to pick it up in half an hour. Fifteen minutes later, the buzzer went. I opened the door and there he was again, with a carrier bag full of steaming, delicious-smelling food. What was his game? I couldn't help smiling, in spite of myself. He asked me what my name was, and I told him I wasn't in the habit of giving my name to delivery boys. He just smiled at my put-down with his cheeky grin, held out his hand and introduced himself.

I relented and said, 'Hello, Mahmoud. I'm Donya.'

He loitered for a few minutes, reluctant to leave, until I said, 'Well, it's been lovely to meet you, Mahmoud, but my food will be getting cold.'

He smiled again and told me he'd see me around, before slipping away into the night.

A few days later, I returned home after a shopping trip with Marlon and called out a greeting to Tracey, who'd been staying with me for a few days. I could hear voices coming from the front room, so I put my head round the door. I could hardly believe my eyes – there was Mahmoud sitting chatting to Tracey. He jumped to his feet and said hello. I felt a little awkward, not knowing what he was doing there, but I tried not to let it show. I introduced him to Marlon, who had been in bed on his previous two visits. He stooped down, shook Marlon's hand in mock seriousness and said, 'Hello, little man. How are you?'

Marlon was very taken with him and responded well. As a single mother, it is warming to see your son with a man when a father-figure is absent from his life. And Mahmoud was playing a good game. Any woman with children makes them her priority, so a good way to her heart is through her kids. That said, Marlon has always bonded very well with Mahmoud and to this day calls him Dad.

I sent Marlon into the kitchen with Tracey to get a glass of milk, turned to Mahmoud and said, 'OK, so what are you doing in my flat?'

He smiled and said, 'I wanted to see you again, Donya. I was wondering whether you would like to go out for lunch with me one day?' I admired his courage.

We agreed a day later in the week and went out together. It was flattering to have male attention again, and we had a great time. Over the next few weeks, we started to see a lot more of each other – going for meals, walks in the park, shopping trips to the West End – and whenever he came to the flat he always behaved very properly with Marlon, who seemed to enjoy having a man around.

Soon, we were embarking on a relationship, and I realised that this man was coming to mean a great deal to me. Having turned down two extremely wealthy men, here I was falling in love with a waiter from a restaurant on Edgware Road. It just goes to prove the wisdom of the old saying that love is blind. Blind, I thought with a smile, and bloody stupid to boot. We had only been seeing each other for a matter of months when I learned that I was pregnant again. We were over the moon.

We decided that we would get married, and set the date. We had a civil ceremony at the Marylebone Register Office, where lots of celebrities have spent part of their wedding days, most famously Paul McCartney and Linda Eastman on 12 March 1969, when the usually jam-packed Marylebone Road had congestion of another sort – it was thronged with hundreds of crying girls, bereft and inconsolable at their true love being snatched away.

In October 1995, less than a week before my 30th birthday, I gave birth to a beautiful blond-haired, green-eyed boy. We named him Khalid, which means 'immortal' in Arabic. Unfortunately, he was anything but. He is frail, often sick, and has terrible stomach problems which have seen us in and out of hospitals over the years. Perhaps it is his familiarity with the medical world that has shaped his ambition – he wants to be a doctor.

With a newborn baby, my flat was too small for us, so we moved to Mahmoud's flat. I hated it. It was in a high-rise block in Southall, a poorer suburb of outer London, not far from Heathrow Airport, with a large immigrant population. I was used to living centrally, and having the West End and Hyde Park on my doorstep. Suddenly, I was having to buy my groceries from a rather shabby street market and had a very different class of neighbour to what I was used to. I'm embarrassed to say that it brought out the snob in me, not that I'm from aristocratic stock myself.

The other problem was that the flat had been left exactly as Mahmoud's first wife had decorated it. Her taste was quite different to mine – all pink shag-pile carpets and PVC furniture (I won't flatter it by using the weasel words 'imitation leather'). It made Rodney and Del Boy Trotter look like they had taste. One of the first things I did was wait until Mahmoud was at work, then pulled up the carpets. I'd hired a van to take them and the revolting furniture away to the rubbish dump. I had ordered a new carpet to be fitted and some furniture to be delivered the same day, so when Mahmoud finally got home from work, the look on his face was comical. It was as though he thought he had walked into the wrong flat. I have always taken the view that it is far easier to get forgiveness than permission and, besides, if I had not taken action, we would probably still be in that awful place to this day. As it was, even with a makeover, I never liked it. We saved up and bought a flat back in my old stomping ground of Maida Vale. It felt like coming home.

Chapter 4

My First Mission

Life continued in reasonably contented domesticity in much the same vein for the next few years. Our first son, Khalid, was followed by a daughter, Amira, then in 1998 came baby Allawi, or Alla, as he instantly became known to us. We carried on living in Maida Vale, and I settled more or less happily into the role of mother. I worshipped my children: wise and sensitive Marlon, the little man of the family; frail little Khalid, who had a dirty-straw head of hair, which is unusual for someone with Arabic blood; my little princess Amira, so bubbly and inquisitive, with her head of curls that she would shake as she laughed happily while we played one of our silly games; and little Allawi. I felt very blessed.

I threw myself into motherhood with energy and enthusiasm, walking the kids to school, collecting them, taking them to the park for the afternoon. In many ways, I was like any one of the many mothers who would gather at the school gate, dressed in the burka, chador or hajib, chattering away in Arabic. The only difference was that I wasn't Arabic, and part of my culture and Western upbringing always served to remind me that there should be more to life. It wasn't that I was in any way unhappy – far from it. I had four wonderful children, a loving husband and a beautiful flat, which I had done everything I could to make as homely and cosy as possible.

It was just that I felt a slight nagging voice, as though someone was tugging at my sleeve every so often, saying, 'Donya, you can do more than this.' It was a vague, unformulated feeling that made me feel ever so slightly dissatisfied, as though I had been put on the earth to do more than this; that if I wasn't careful I, already moving towards my mid-30s, would end up letting life slip by. But, of course, like so many stay-at-home mothers, I ignored it and concentrated on my duties to my husband and children, telling myself I should count my blessings. There were so many other women less fortunate than me, I told myself – those who had an abusive husband, for example, or wanted children but couldn't have them.

And then I met Mary.

One afternoon, I took the children on a shopping trip down to Queensway, one of my favourite places in London. It is like being in the Middle East, with brightly lit shops open all hours; grocers with tables outside, groaning under the weight of exotic fruit and vegetables; Middle Eastern restaurants, from which waft the delicious smells of spiced meats . . . I was at a bus stop with my bags and my army of children, who were by now complaining and wanting their tea, waiting to go home. As I juggled bags and kids, I noticed a woman next to me who must have seen the exasperation etched on my face. Like so many other women in that area, she was also a British Muslim, but dressed very drably; she had a downtrodden air about her that made me take pity on her instantly. I took her look to be one of sympathy from one mother to another.

'They can be such a handful, can't they?' I said as a pleasantry. She nodded her assent without speaking. 'Do you have any yourself?' I continued.

She replied that she did, a little girl of six, or coming up to it, and

I asked where she was. It was a normal school day, so it seemed unusual that her daughter wouldn't be with her. I certainly couldn't even go to the corner shop without undertaking a quasi-military operation, grappling with pushchairs, overcoats, hats, gloves, you name it. Perhaps, underneath, I was slightly jealous of her freedom. To my alarm, though, the woman's eyes filled with tears.

'She's in Libya,' she managed to say. 'Her father took her there six months ago.'

I had a horrible feeling I knew what was coming next. Although it hadn't happened to anyone in my immediate circle, living in a mixed British and Muslim community meant that I had heard of similar cases, and thanked God that it hadn't happened to anyone close to me.

'Do you get to speak to her?' I asked as gently as I could.

She broke down and started to sob, saying she didn't, that the girl's father wouldn't allow her to speak to her mother, no matter how often she rang, pleading for the chance just to hear her little girl's voice. I was shocked. Surrounded by my kids, as I was, the idea of not being able to touch them, kiss them, drop them off and pick them up from school, or tuck them up in bed at night seemed incomprehensible. That someone would prevent a mother from even speaking to her daughter seemed criminal and cruel to the point of being evil.

At that moment, our bus came, and I had my hands full trying to shepherd my little flock onto the busy gangway while trying to manhandle a pushchair on board. When I looked behind me, the woman had gone, melted into the crowds.

However, our chance meeting had really made a deep impact upon me. It is one thing to read about things such as this happening in the newspapers, or hearing about it third-, fourth- or fifth-hand, as having befallen a stranger at the peripheries of the community in which you live, but to be confronted with it so unexpectedly, in such an everyday setting, to see the lines of pain and sorrow drawn so deep on another human being's face was truly a shock.

That evening, I discussed it with Mahmoud. As ever, he was gentle and understanding, but he couldn't see why it had affected me so much. 'Donya,' he said, 'these things happen in the world. It can be a bad place. Why are you letting it upset you so much?'

It was a good question. I could watch the news and see images of a horrendous train crash, or a child that had been killed by a hit-and-run driver, without letting it affect me personally. Of course, it is upsetting to see these stories, and you can imagine the pain that other distant, nameless, faceless families must be enduring, but you just get on with your life. This chance encounter had touched me in a far more intimate way; it was almost as though this stranger's grief should somehow be something I could share or try to resolve.

Looking back, I think there were a couple of reasons for this. The first was the fact that she, like me, was a British Muslim, a woman who had been brought up with liberal Western values, but who had chosen to marry a Muslim man. The two worlds are so different that I felt that I, more than other people, could understand the pain caused when the tension between the two cultures became too great and things fell apart. What had shocked me, I suppose, was suddenly being aware of the cost in human terms. I had only ever thought about such situations in a very abstract way, if I had ever really thought about them at all. I was being forced to think about what that actually meant: a mother, old beyond her years, worn down and oppressed by the terrible, cruel blow that fate had dealt her; a little girl suddenly uprooted from her school, her home, her mother, her friends, her life in busy, cosmopolitan London and snatched away to go and start all over again in a village where everyone speaks a different language, with no mum to soothe her, cuddle her or tell her it's going to be all right.

Then there was possibly the guilt that I felt at some level over what I had done to Marlon's father, Theo. Why was that so different to what a man had done to this poor woman, this act that I saw as abhorrent and unspeakable? I suppose my way of rationalising it was to reaffirm my unshakeable belief that a child should never be separated from its mother.

Another factor was that I was, of course, married to a Muslim from another part of the world. While Mahmoud had always been a gentle, kind and considerate husband and father, it was also true that this woman would probably have once said the same thing about her husband – and yet he had kidnapped her daughter and taken her back to Libya. Who was to say that my own husband was not capable of doing the same thing?

Many Arab men who come to London are initially seduced by the liberal values of the West. They come from a culture where women cover themselves up and remain apart from male company until they marry. Not only is sex before marriage out of the question, even socialising with women of their own age is generally taboo. It must be a heady, intoxicating brew suddenly to find yourself in a social cauldron like London. Women are supposedly 'liberated', sexually precocious and sophisticated. There is more flesh on show simply walking through the streets than at a halal meat market back home. Girls wear miniskirts with crop tops that expose their midriffs, and have their navels pierced. Often women make the first move, and for those that want it, sex is freely available. After the restrictions of home, it must be incredibly seductive.

But as time goes by, these temptations soon appear shallow and meaningless. For many of these men, particularly when they have a daughter, the values of the West come to seem pernicious. They worry that their children will grow up to inherit certain loose, immoral values prevalent in the West.

A good example of these supposedly immoral attitudes came in the form of Becki Seddiki, one of the contestants on Channel 4's *Big Brother* reality-TV show. Moroccan-born but a resident of the UK, her exploits inside the house included toe-sucking, flashing her surgically enhanced boobs, licking jam from another contestant's breasts and pretending to perform oral sex on a cucumber. So far, so zany – and, of course, no big deal to anyone brought up on a diet of Western titillation and sauciness. The UK is a country, after all, whose best-selling daily newspaper still includes pictures of topless women on Page 3.

But poor Becki hadn't reckoned on the Muslim backlash that her antics would cause, with hardliners interpreting her behaviour as a slur which brought disgrace on their religion. Her elderly parents, Ahmed and Fatima, disowned her. They refused to have anything to do with her, which is, of course, a tragedy in itself, but far worse were stories that relatives back home in Morocco were reportedly so incensed by what the self-confessed former belly-dancer had done that they issued death threats, like the fatwa against Salman Rushdie – all the poor girl had done was take part in some tacky, juvenile game show. It was crazy.

It is in this context that you have to judge the behaviour of some Arab fathers living in the West. It's very hypocritical, but that's the way it is. Many of them are happy to come and cavort in the fleshpots of cities like London, hanging out with women, drinking and gambling. If you go to any of the casinos in the capital's exclusive Mayfair district, well over half the clientele will be Arabs, drinking and womanising. But for these men, or some of them at least, once they have had their fun in the West, maybe had a daughter, they suddenly despair of its immorality and fear that their little girl will grow up to take drugs, get drunk and sleep around. Once this pathological hatred of the West sets in, nothing will change their outlook. The child's mother is included in this sweeping condemnation of all that the West stands for. In the man's view, she is tainted beyond redemption. This is when some fathers become dangerous. Their thinking is that they must abduct their child before it is irrevocably poisoned by the Sodom-like immorality in which they are growing up.

I've seen it all so many times now that I am often called upon to share my experience in this field on television shows, and in newspaper and magazine articles. But back then, in 1998, I was only just awakening; it was as though the scales were only just beginning to fall from my eyes. Deep inside me, I felt a stirring, perhaps the beginning of a calling. When I look back, this was the pivotal moment that changed my life almost beyond recognition, and helped me to discover what it was that I had been put on the earth to do.

And, sure enough, fate intervened again. About five months later, I took the children down to Hyde Park, just a bus ride from where we were living. As I walked through the park, I saw this woman again. She recognised me, and we started to chat. But with four children to look after, I couldn't concentrate. I suggested to her that we meet for a coffee the next day, and she readily agreed.

The next morning, I set off with a spring in my step – it was as though I had some sense of the momentous change in direction that my life was about to take, yet I had no idea at the time. I headed down to Queensway once more. We had arranged to meet in Whiteleys, in Bayswater, my favourite shopping centre. It was once an enormous Victorian department store – its motto: 'Everything from a Pin to an Elephant' – and its handsome façade remains to this day. Inside, however, it has been modernised, but it's still very light and airy, thanks to its glass roof.

We had arranged to meet at 11 a.m. at Café Rouge on the second floor. I arrived dead on the hour and, sure enough, my new-found friend was already there waiting for me. Her face lit up when she saw me – I guess she didn't have too many people to talk to about her tragedy. I ordered a coffee, pulled up a chair and began to listen. We were still there when they were clearing tables after their busy lunch period.

Her name was Mary, she told me, and she had married a Libyan man. Her story followed that of so many women whom I would come to know, and to help, over the years which followed. To begin with, everything had been fine. She had even gone to Libya when they first married to meet his family and was given a rapturous welcome. When they returned to England, she had been a good and dutiful Muslim wife, wearing traditional dress, and eschewing her former friends and Western lifestyle. Nonetheless, her husband still constantly found grounds to chide and criticise her. They had a little girl, whom they called Leila.

It had been almost a year since Mary had gone to collect Leila from school that day. She stood in the playground with the other mothers as the children swarmed out from the school, but she couldn't see Leila, who was normally one of the first to come running up to the group of mums. Soon all the mothers had picked up their children and left, leaving Mary standing alone in the playground. A teacher came over and explained that her husband had taken Leila out of school that morning to attend a dentist's appointment.

Mary was shocked, but had tried not to show it. Her husband was not the sort of man who had ever got involved in the practical side of parenting, leaving all that to Mary. She pretended to the teacher that it had slipped her mind, thanked her and went home. Inside, she was in turmoil. What could it mean? By the time it had grown dark, she was frantic with worry. She began calling all her husband's friends, asking whether they had seen him and Leila. Eventually, one of them took pity on her and told her that he had taken Leila back to Libya, saying that it was probably for a holiday and he was sure they would be back soon.

As Mary told me her story, tears were running down her cheeks, something that I would come to witness again and again over the years. No matter how old the wound is, for these mothers it always seems raw and fresh. I couldn't help but contrast this behaviour as I saw more and more of these cases with the men's actions, which always seemed to be calculated, cold and cruel, and had been planned over months. To me, the motivation of the men sprang in part from cruelty and hatred – hatred of the West, hatred of their wives, whatever – while the acts of the women generally seemed to spring from love. You may think this is an oversimplification, but it is partly what lies at the bottom of my firm belief that a mother should never be separated from her children. In the rarest of cases, it is better if custody is awarded to the father – but I emphasise that this is only in the very rarest of cases and is the exception that proves the rule.

Mary went on to explain that she had called her husband's family in Libya repeatedly. The reception she got contrasted starkly with the effusive welcome she had received when she first visited them. They were guarded and mistrustful and spitefully refused to allow her to speak to her daughter. To begin with, they would invent excuses – 'Leila is too tired to talk' or 'Leila is playing at a friend's house' – but eventually they just said, 'You will never speak to Leila. Forget you had a daughter.'

At least they were being honest, I suppose. When the phone number Mary had for them stopped working, Mary had to face the fact they'd moved without telling her. The psychological umbilical cord had finally been cut, in the cruellest way imaginable.

During one of our meetings, on a sudden impulse I leaned forward and said to Mary, 'Why don't we go to Libya and snatch Leila back? It's the only way you'll ever get to see her again.'

Mary was shocked, but I convinced her we could do it. How difficult could it be? It was a decision that was to change my life.

I was full of excitement at the fledgling plan we were hatching. I felt alive in a way that I hadn't done for years. The crazy antics that had marked my youth had, it seemed with hindsight, sprung from a need for adrenalin, for excitement. Misguided though they were, they attested to a part of my personality that needed drama and action. It was as though I had now found a way of satisfying that craving in a positive way, one that actually benefited the world, rather than one that, at best, hurt other people and, at worst, could have seen me in prison. It hadn't yet occurred to me that this modern-day Florence Nightingale routine could have the same results – and indeed would some way down the line. There was one fly in the ointment, though: what the hell was I going to tell Mahmoud?

'Donya, you are going to do what? Are you mad? What's going to happen to our children while you go off on this wild-goose chase? And what if they catch you? Libya isn't Britain, they'll throw you in prison.' Mahmoud couldn't believe his ears. The annoying thing was that, deep down, I knew he was right. Still, once I have decided on a course of action, nobody can talk me out of it. I'm very stubborn like that. Eventually, Mahmoud realised that he couldn't say anything that would change my mind, and it was arranged that Mary and I would fly out to Libya and look for Leila.

She bought tickets for us and we went down to Heathrow for the first of what would turn out to be many of these trips over the years. As well as the obvious danger of what we were planning, there was an added risk. As we knew we would not be able to get hold of Leila's passport, we had decided that Mary should travel on her sister's. She had a daughter who was named on her passport, so Leila would be able to get out of Libya and back into the UK – but only if the passport officials were not too alert. It was a huge risk, but one that we had to take.

I felt an instant buzz as we arrived at the airport in Tripoli, Libya's bustling capital. I have always loved the excitement of being in an Arabic country where everything is so different. Even the boards that announce departures and arrivals seem exotic, with their Arabic writing. It's like another world. The grave nature of our undertaking didn't detract from the excitement – indeed, in many ways, it simply served to add to it. But, of course, we were on a mission, and we needed to be focused. The first thing was to get out of the airport and find a driver who could help us.

The fact that I spoke some Arabic was an enormous bonus. Once outside, I was able to go up to a gaggle of taxi drivers and start haggling. I explained that we needed a driver for two or three days' work and one said that he was available. We settled on a price of $20 per day, which was very cheap by British standards. Mary had managed to find out some details of Leila's whereabouts from friends in London, so we headed to the small town and soon identified the house. It was evening by now and there was nothing more we could do for that day. We found a small, cheap hotel and took a room, sharing to save money.

Our plan for the following morning was to park down the road from the house, so that we could discreetly keep an eye on the comings and goings. Our driver was parked outside asleep in the car – our budget didn't cover accommodation for him, but he seemed perfectly happy and cheerful. I tried to imagine asking the same sort of service from a London taxi driver and laughed to myself at the idea. They won't even agree to go south of the river if it doesn't suit them, let alone sleep in their taxi outside a hotel for the night as they waited at their customers' beck and call.

We got into position in good time, before there was any sign of life from the house. At around 8 a.m., an ancient and battered school bus pulled up outside. Mary automatically sat bolt upright as the front door opened and a small girl appeared with her books, running out to get on the bus.

'That's her!' she exclaimed, her hand automatically reaching for the door handle.

I restrained her. 'Not now, Mary,' I urged. 'It's too dangerous. Let's just follow and work out the routine. Once we have a plan, then we'll act. OK?'

'OK,' she agreed reluctantly, settling back into her seat. We followed the bus and when it pulled up at the school gate we parked a few hundred yards away. I watched intently, trying to take everything in. On the plus side, as with all schools, there was a degree of pandemonium, which suited us well, as it would afford us some cover. As well as the bus, there were dozens of cars pulling up, disgorging their occupants for school. On the minus side, there was a teacher at the school gate, keeping an eye on everything and seeming to count the children in.

We spent the whole day in the car. Our driver very kindly went off every so often to fetch us something to eat or drink. I wanted to see if there would be any time during the day when the children were taken out of the school, perhaps to a field for sport – just something out of the ordinary which would offer us an opportunity to grab Leila. Of course, no such thing happened. The first sign of any activity was at the end of the school day, when the bus pulled up once again, and the children streamed out of the building, some boarding the bus, others getting into cars which had arrived to collect them.

We followed the bus back to the house where Leila was staying. She skipped off the bus, ran up to the front door and was let in. We carried on watching for several more hours, but apart from lights coming on as it grew dark, there was nothing to see. We went back to our hotel and had an early night, shattered from the day's surveillance.

The next morning, it was the same routine. Once again, we followed the bus to school, once again we sat outside all day, once again we followed the bus home. It all happened in exactly the same way as the previous day. That night in the hotel we discussed what we were going to do. We were booked on a flight back to the UK the following day, and Mary's modest funds were almost exhausted. We had to move.

'The only chance we have is in the morning,' I argued. 'You have to get to Leila as she gets off the bus and then we go.'

'But there are so many people around,' said Mary. 'How can we take her from right under their noses?'

I conceded that it was tricky, but I couldn't see that we had any other option. We would have to have faith and hope that God was on our side. It was difficult to sleep that night, knowing what the morning would bring, but I eventually dropped off.

Before I knew it, the alarm was going. It was time to put our crazy plan into action. We followed the bus as on the previous two days, but this time, we pulled up right beside it, near to the school.

'This is it,' I said to Mary. 'Go and get your daughter.'

Mary was wearing traditional dress, so she didn't stand out. I watched as Leila came down the steps of the bus. Mary stooped down to her, and Leila threw her arms round her. The two of them stood embracing like that for what seemed like an eternity. I began to panic. They would surely draw attention to themselves. The teacher by the school gate would see them any second.

Cursing, I got out of the car and went straight up to the teacher. I told her that I had just moved to the area and was looking for a school for my little girl. It seemed to distract her for a moment. Very politely, she explained the procedure, that I should ring the school office to make an appointment, then I would be very welcome to come back, with my little girl if I so wished, and they would happily show us around.

Out of the corner of my eye, I could see that Mary and Leila had at last got into the car. I thanked the woman for her time, feeling a tiny prick of conscience at the deception I had played, then got into the car. We sped off, trying to get away from the school as quickly as we could before the alarm was raised.

Beside me, Mary was embracing Leila as though she would never let her go, drinking in every detail of her like someone who is given water after a long, thirsty trek; tears were running down her face. I had to think quickly. It was several hours' driving back to Tripoli, so I asked the driver if there was an airport nearby from where we could catch a plane. He said that there was, and we headed straight there. It was a small, provincial airport, but nonetheless there seemed to be quite a few officials about, which made me feel tense. For all I knew, the alarm had already been raised and airports had been warned to be on the lookout.

I told Mary to stay in the car with Leila while I tried to get flights for us. I approached the desk and asked when the next flight would be. The booking assistant spread his arms in apology and explained that there had been a delay. The next flight would not be for several hours. I thanked him and went back to the car.

We couldn't risk waiting, so I spoke to the driver, who agreed the safest option was to drive to Morocco and fly home from there.

He would take us all the way to the border with Algeria, from where we would pick up another car. It would be less dangerous than staying there and perhaps getting caught. After 17 hot, dusty hours, we arrived at the border. My heart was in my mouth as the guard inspected our papers, but after a moment's perfunctory checking, he simply waved us through.

Our driver found someone to take over from him, and after saying thank you and paying him his money, we switched cars. The next driver was to take us the hundreds of miles across Algeria into Morocco. Despite being an area constantly listed by the Foreign Office as too dangerous for travellers, I felt we had no option. If it meant we could reach Morocco and fly home, it was surely a risk worth taking. I had convinced myself that, as well as notifying ports and airports in Libya, the authorities would notify those of neighbouring countries. There was no way they would expect us to drive all the way to Morocco – or at least that's what I was banking on.

I was in such an agitated state that I'm not even sure which airport we eventually arrived at. The stress of what we had done, added to the fatigue of being in a car without air conditioning for hour upon hour on dusty roads was taking its toll. But the plan seemed to work, in so far as we encountered no problems at the airport.

Even when we were on the plane, though, I couldn't relax. We still had the biggest hurdle of all to negotiate – UK Immigration at Heathrow. When we landed, we joined the line of bedraggled arrivals from North Africa queuing to clear passport control. The officials seemed far more thorough than those in Libya and Morocco. I suppose it's more common that people from these countries try to get into the UK illegally than the other way around. Would they spot that Mary was travelling on her sister's passport? I held my breath as we went through. The woman glanced down, then at Mary and Leila. This was it, the moment of truth. She smiled, handed back the passports and said, 'Thank you, Madam.' We had done it.

I had phoned Mahmoud from Morocco to tell him when we would be landing, and my face lit up when I saw him waiting for us, with a quizzical smile. We climbed into his car and headed back into London. Mary and Leila got out by a Tube station, and we embraced, then she disappeared with Leila into the crowd. She has since wisely changed her name and moved house.

I have never heard from her again and could not get in touch with her if I wanted to. I hope and believe that she is living happily with Leila in another part of the country, and if she by chance should be reading this, I send her my love and best wishes. She was a very brave and determined woman who inspired me to take the first step down the road which led me to where I am today, and for that I salute her.

Chapter 5

A Growing Reputation

.

One of the benefits, and an occasional drawback, of living in a close-knit community such as the Middle Eastern one that I was part of in west London is that each individual is very visible. I already stood out, thanks to being one of only a small number of British Muslims. Now, thanks to what I had done with Mary, I became a minor celebrity. I didn't broadcast what had happened. It was controversial and, of course, illegal. In the same way that men taking children from Britain back to the Middle East flies in the face of public opinion and criminal law in the UK, the exact opposite – that is, women taking their children away to bring them home to the West – was true in the Middle East. The culture was such that society in general, and the courts in particular, favoured the rights of the father over the mother. The fact that, in many cases, the mother might have a UK court ruling in her favour would carry no weight. Just as we term it 'child abduction' or 'kidnapping', so too would the Libyan authorities, and if I had been caught, I would have been labelled an accomplice, or possibly deemed part of a conspiracy, as the whole thing had been planned in advance and was not an impulsive crime of passion.

In addition to the stigma I had attracted through my possible criminal activity, the community would have taken a dim view of my actions. While few would agree with what Leila's father had done, there was a powerful overriding belief that you don't get involved in other people's business. The fact that I was a woman, and a British woman at that, poking my nose into another man's business would have been controversial. For that reason, I told few people about what I had done. Nonetheless, word somehow seemed to spread. The handful of close friends I took into my confidence clearly told a handful of their acquaintances, and they in turn told theirs, until soon it seemed as though the whole world knew about it.

What surprised me, though, was the fact that, far from being shunned, or worse, many Muslim women came up and congratulated me. It was as though there was a silent majority of Muslim women who disapproved of the chauvinistic nature of some aspects of Islam. There were even some men who told me that they admired my actions – although that was generally when no one else was around to witness it.

The upshot was that, every so often, a mother would come up to me, often when I was standing at the school gate waiting for the children, and tell me quietly about the predicament of a friend of a friend who'd found herself in the same situation as Mary. These conversations were often hurried and told in low, murmuring voices in case anyone overheard. I began to think that child abduction was British Islam's dirty secret – known about but covered up by the community. It wasn't surprising – Muslims in the UK have enough prejudice to contend with; there was little point in giving further ammunition to racists and bigots.

Although at first I was reluctant to get involved, soon the injustice of these situations served to fuel my indignation, and I felt that I could not ignore these pleas. It seemed as though God had put me on this earth for a reason, and if my role was to bridge the gap between East and West in these tug-of-love cases, perhaps I should start to think about what I could do to help. My familiarity with Islam and Arabic on the one hand, and my Western upbringing and exposure to equal rights for men and women on the other put me in a unique position.

My trip to Libya to rescue Leila had taken place in late 1998 when Allawi was still a baby. Sometime in the spring of 1999, I was approached by a friend of a friend called Debbie. Her story was in many ways similar to Mary's. I agreed to meet her at 'the office', which is how I had started to refer to Café Rouge at Whiteleys.

What she told me was no less heartbreaking for following the same pattern as others. No matter how many times I am told these tragic tales, they remain as shocking and cruel each time. The snatch was similar to Leila's; her daughter had also been taken out of school on a fictitious appointment. And, like Mary, by the time Debbie had realised what had happened, her little girl, Amina, had been spirited out of the country, in this case to Morocco.

If there is any message I can impart to mothers at risk of this happening, it is this: watch out for unusual patterns of behaviour. If, after a long period of dissent from and unhappiness with your husband, you find that he has suddenly become kind and solicitous to help out with the kids, offering to bath them and take them to the park, where previously he has left all that kind of thing to you, alarm bells should be ringing. Make sure you know where your children's passports are at all times. If you suddenly can't find a favourite top or teddy bear, you are in danger. He is probably taking things out of the home a little at a time and keeping them at the home of a so-called friend – or accomplice, as I prefer to call that person. This is to make the departure easier. He will not want to have a reluctant, crying child drawing attention to him at the airport. By having familiar toys and clothes with him, he'll think he stands a better chance of placating the children and slipping out of the country.

If you have recognised any of the above patterns of behaviour, you must move quickly. Explain your fears to the school your children attend; tell them that if the father ever turns up to take them to a doctor's appointment of which they have had no prior notification, they are not to let the child go without clearing it with you. If you have concrete evidence, such as flight tickets that you've found, immediately ring your local police station and ask to be put through to the child-protection unit. Forewarned is forearmed.

Poor Debbie, though, had not read the signs until it was too late. And her case differed from that of Mary in one crucial way – she had never been to meet her partner's family in Morocco, and realised he hadn't left anything behind which would provide an address or any way of getting in touch. Even his surname was a common one. We were talking about trying to find a needle in a haystack. I reluctantly told her that there was nothing I could do. I urged her to speak to her husband's friends to try to get an address or something that we could go on, but sobbing, she shook her head. She explained that her husband had never really introduced her to his friends, and the one or two that she did know refused to help. The community, as is often the case, had closed ranks against her, shutting her out. I could do nothing. With a heavy heart, I gave her my phone number and told her to get in touch if anything should change. Feeling a great sadness, I watched her leave, then set off home myself to my own children. I didn't expect to hear from her again.

Then, a few weeks later, Debbie rang in a state of great excitement. A friend of hers had just rung from Morocco, where she was on holiday. She was convinced that she had just seen Amina at a beach resort. There was no time to lose. If she was there visiting with her father, she could be leaving any day. We had to get out there – and quickly. I explained to Mahmoud what I was about to do, and he accepted it with weary resignation. He knew better than to try to talk me out of it.

We got flights to Morocco the next day and soon arrived at the resort. We booked into a hotel and went out onto the room's balcony, where the scale of the task became apparent. The beach was enormous and packed with holidaymakers – older women in traditional dress sitting chatting while their youngsters played. It seemed hopeless. But Debbie leaned on the balcony rail and scanned the crowd intently. This went on for at least a couple of hours.

I tried to suggest that we would be better off going down to the beach and wandering about, looking at close range, but she was having none of it, waving me away impatiently when I suggested it. My fear was that, since it was now late afternoon, the sun would soon start going down, and everyone would pack up and leave the beach. If this happened, we would lose a day, and for all we knew they could be leaving that night, if they hadn't already done so. I thought how futile it all was. Why didn't I listen to Mahmoud more?

But then Debbie gave a whoop. I rushed back out to the balcony.

'There,' she cried, pointing. 'That's Amina there!' I tried to follow, but all I could see were masses of people. 'She's with three women and those other children. They're sitting on the chairs and she's running down to the water with a red rubber ring.'

We decided to head down with headscarves on, so we didn't stand out too much. Then, with my Arabic, I could try to talk to the women and see what I could find out. Debbie would have to stay in the background. The plan worked well. I sat near the women and could see that one of them, the oldest of the group, was keeping an eye on little Amina as she splashed about in the shallow water. I struck up conversation with the old woman, complimenting her on her little girl. She told me proudly that she was her granddaughter. It was clear that she loved her, and I felt bad, realising the heartache that I had come to cause in Morocco. It was a feeling that I would experience many times over the years. These tug-of-love cases are always heartbreaking, as there is rarely a black-and-white answer. The only way I have found to deal with the guilt is to stay focused on the practical job in hand and remember that my role is to reunite a child with its mother. But sometimes it is hard.

The old woman explained that they were there on holiday and that they would be leaving in two days. As we chatted, Amina ran up. Her grandmother told her that it was time to start packing up her things. Amina pouted and said that she didn't want to leave the beach, but her grandmother placated her by promising they could come back for the whole of the next day. I bade her goodbye and headed off, nodding to Debbie to follow.

Once we were back at the hotel, I told her what I had learned. 'Right, tomorrow is the day. It will be their last day on the beach before they go home and we have to be ready to move.'

Debbie was happy to go along with what I was arranging, happy to let me take control. It was hard to sleep that night – it always is before an attempted rescue, as a mixture of fear of being caught and adrenalin takes over – but eventually I managed.

The next morning, I approached a driver and explained that I would pay him for a whole day if he kept himself free and ensured that he could arrive within a few minutes of my call. He was more than happy to be given a day's pay at full rate for one little job and gave me his phone number. We took up position on the balcony and started to watch for Amina arriving with her grandmother and relatives. When we saw them, it was time to move.

Once again, we wrapped up and headed down to take up a spot close enough to them to be able to keep an eye on proceedings, but not so near as to draw attention to ourselves. We were both tense and the minutes seemed to drag by. We had taken the precaution of booking return flights that afternoon, and the clock was ticking. After a couple of hours, the women began to discuss what they would have for lunch. There was a sandwich bar behind us, where the beach met the road, and it was clear that they were planning to go there. I took it all in. Amina was still paddling down in the shallow waves by herself. We had a window of opportunity. While the women ambled back to the sandwich bar, their backs turned to the water, we would have a couple of minutes as they got their food and returned to the beach.

It was now or never. As they got up, I whispered to Debbie, 'OK, this is it. Go and get Amina, take her back to the hotel room and ring the driver to come and get us. I'll join you there.' She needed no second bidding. I watched as she ran down to Amina, bent down and pulled back her veil. The little girl's face lit up, and she jumped into her mother's arms. As they hugged, I panicked. They needed to get moving before anyone noticed anything untoward. I was willing them to walk away. After what felt like an eternity, but was probably only a few seconds, they walked off, Debbie carrying Amina, who had her arms round her mother's neck, beaming away. Then it was as though they had never been there.

From behind, Debbie just looked like another Muslim woman in her long, shapeless dress. She strode off in the opposite direction to the sandwich bar and left the beach, joining all the other people walking along the pavement by the seafront road. A moment later, the women returned with their sandwiches and sat down, handing them out. They chatted among themselves, but I could see that the grandmother was looking down to the water where the little girl had been.

'Where's Amina?' she said.

No one took any notice until she said it a second time, this time with urgency in her voice. They all peered in the same direction, then slowly got to their feet. By now, they were beginning to panic. They strode down to the water, calling the little girl's name. Others around me began to take notice. We didn't have long.

In the confusion, I slipped away and headed back to the hotel. Debbie and Amina were in the room, cuddling each other and laughing happily. One look at my face, though, told Debbie the time to celebrate was yet to come. I asked whether she had phoned the driver. She said that she had, but that he would be around half an hour. I cursed, but there was nothing I could do. I packed the bags and told them to wait in the room until I rang and called them down. I didn't want them sitting in reception while the cry went up for a missing girl.

I took the bags down and sat on a sofa in the lobby, growing more and more anxious. Looking out of the window, the commotion was evident. Police cars were arriving and the beach was a scene of pandemonium. Where the hell was that driver? At last, he sauntered in without a care in the world, mumbling some rubbish about traffic in response to my barked questions about where he had been and why he had taken so long to arrive. It couldn't be helped. I called Debbie and Amina down, and we bundled into the car, keeping Amina's head well down as we drove past the police cars. Now our enemy was time – our flight was in two hours and the driver told us it was well over an hour to the airport.

I told him he'd get a fat bonus if he got us there as quickly as possible, and he put his foot down. An hour later, we were rushing up to check in. We had made it.

Sitting back in my seat as the aeroplane hurtled down the runway, I looked across at Debbie as she beamed away proudly, ruffling her little girl's hair. It was a look I had seen on Mary's face, and would see again and again over the years. It was what made it all – the fear, the self-doubts, the guilt – completely and undeniably worthwhile.

Chapter 6

In-laws and Outlaws

Over the next few years, my reputation as a woman who was prepared to get her hands dirty in international tug-of-love cases grew. Many of the women whom I came to hear of and meet were, literally, at their wits' end. The problem for many is that, although they take their cases to court in the UK and win the right to have their children returned, UK law holds little or no sway in the countries to which their estranged husbands and partners have taken the children, invariably in the Middle East and North Africa.

The key international law relating to abducted children is the Hague Convention. In 1976, at the lead and instigation of, among others, Canada and the UK, a conference on international private law was held. One of the aims was to agree to a treaty that would be incorporated into member countries' domestic law. One of the key ideas of the convention has been summarised as follows:

> The Hague Convention is a civil legal mechanism available
> to parents seeking the return of, or access to, their child. As
> a civil law mechanism, the parents, not the governments, are
> parties to the legal action.
>
> The countries that are party to the Convention have

agreed that a child who is habitually resident in one party country, and who has been removed to or retained in another party country in violation of the left-behind parent's custodial rights, shall be promptly returned to the country of habitual residence. The convention can also help parents exercise visitation rights abroad.

This was an important step forward. It meant for the first time that the onus was on the foreign government to retrieve children who had been taken from their country of residence, not the wronged parent. So, if a child was taken to a country that was a signatory of the convention, in theory, that country's legal system and police force should seek to find the child and return it to its original country. But it was only a step in the right direction, not the be-all and end-all.

There are two main problems. First, the convention only takes effect if the countries involved are signatories. After the treaty had been drafted and was ready to be signed on 1 July 1988, the countries which endorsed it included the US, the UK, Canada, Australia, France and Spain – none of the women I have helped have ever had their children taken to these countries. The convention is not recognised in most of the Middle East, Asia or Africa, so it could not be called upon to help these poor mothers. And if they tried to pursue their claim through the courts of these lands, they would not get very far with Islamic shariah law generally favouring the rights of the father. Efforts by a mother to bring an action for custody of her child in a court in an Islamic country usually have little prospect of success, especially if she is a foreigner and not a Muslim. Only if the father has grossly neglected his duties – by failing to take care of his child, for instance – does the mother have a slightly better chance in some Islamic states.

Second, just because a country has signed up to the convention, there is no guarantee that there will be any efforts to enforce it. I once helped a woman called Alison Lalic to track down her children, a story I will tell later in this book. In her case, the children had been taken back to the father's homeland of Bosnia–Herzegovina.

Bosnia ratified the Hague Convention on 1 December 1991, along with Croatia, Macedonia, Yugoslavia and Israel, but it may simply have been window-dressing. The Bosnian authorities certainly do not seem to have taxed themselves finding her children – they attended school and could therefore have been found quite easily if the desire and political will had been there.

In the face of such sluggish efforts by the authorities to reunite mother and child, I stepped into the breach. As with Mary and Debbie, it seemed to me the only way to get anything done was to take positive action, and over the next few years, I undertook around 20 of these missions.

Although a mission is life or death for the mother involved and, as I said earlier, each is as heartbreaking as the next in its own way, two of my missions were to be very important and have further ramifications. These were cases involving Mahmoud's sister Ibtihal and then later a case involving a mother called Sarra Fotheringham.

Ibtihal lived in Najaf in southern Iraq, but was tired of the privations and lack of opportunities that were commonplace under Saddam Hussein's regime. She had heard all about Mahmoud's new life in the UK and, like many who seek to leave an oppressive regime and find work opportunities, she decided to join him. The problem was that she could not get a visa. The Government had clamped down on immigration and it was increasingly difficult to get into the UK. I have no political axe to grind, and, of course, I can see that there must be some restraints on immigration – this is a small island and the huge tide of humanity must be controlled, otherwise many from the developing world would want to come here. Having said that, when it comes to individual cases, I'd like to help and don't feel comfortable refusing people who want a better life, and to come to Britain to work and contribute to the economy.

Mahmoud and I talked about it at length. There are people who, in return for large sums of money, will arrange false papers and visas to get you into a country. There are no guarantees, though, and these people-traffickers, as they are called, are extremely unscrupulous, profiting hugely out of other people's desperation and misery.

In 2000, the year Ibtihal was to come to the UK, 60 Chinese immigrants paid large amounts of money to be smuggled into the UK port of Dover from Zeebrugge in Belgium in the back of a lorry. The Dutch lorry driver closed the air vents to prevent Customs officials hearing any noise from the refugees inside. Tragically, when they reached Dover and the lorry was inspected, all but two had died of suffocation.

At the driver's trial, a Chinese immigrant who had arrived in the UK by the same means explained how it worked. After making it to the UK, he was taken to a high-rise block of council flats somewhere in London, where he was kept prisoner by the traffickers, members of a Chinese gang called the Snakeheads, until his family back in China had paid as much as £20,000 for his release. To put it in context, this was described as being the equivalent of 17 years' salary back in China. So these are the sort of people you can end up dealing with when you pay money to be smuggled into the UK.

I had a better idea. Many readers will disapprove of what I did, but I knew how unhappy Ibtihal was in Iraq and how she longed for a better life in the UK. It is easy enough to get to mainland Europe from the Middle East by travelling through Turkey, Greece and Germany, but from western Europe it is virtually impossible to travel on to the UK. The really desperate sometimes try to cling to freight trains travelling through the Channel Tunnel from France, but it is a risky, even life-threatening option.

My plan was far simpler. Mahmoud took some convincing, but

there was no great risk. If Ibtihal could make her way to France or Holland, I would arrange for a friend to meet her with my passport. She could then use that to come into the UK. Officials rarely do anything more than glance at my passport, so we were sure it would work. I had heard of people using the same scam to get into the country and didn't allow myself to consider the possibility of it not working. The penalty for travelling under a false passport was sure to be serious, perhaps even a jail sentence, but I put such thoughts out of my mind.

Ibtihal had two sons, but it was arranged that only one would come with her to avoid arousing suspicion. Her husband and Yussuf, her younger son, who was six years old, would have to try to find a way of coming later.

As I do not wish to jeopardise anybody who helped, I will not go into any detail except to say that the plan worked. Ibtihal made it safely to the UK and found work and somewhere to live. But with her younger son still stuck in Iraq, she was growing increasingly desperate to see him. Her husband had applied for permission to enter the UK, but there was delay after delay, with no guarantee that they would ever get the necessary visas. Eventually, in the summer of 2001, after a year of watching her grow increasingly depressed at being parted from Yussuf, I decided it was time to intervene again.

I told her that we had no choice but to go out to Iraq and get him. As Ibtihal was an illegal immigrant, she could not travel with us. I would go with a friend, collect Yussuf and bring him home.

Mahmoud burst out laughing when I told him my plan. 'That's not going to work, Donya,' he said. 'For one thing, he doesn't have a British passport.'

'He can travel on Khalid's,' I said, without really thinking it through. 'They're roughly the same age.'

Mahmoud thought for a moment. 'That's not going to work. They'll see that Khalid didn't travel out with you, there won't be any stamps in the passport.'

He had a point. 'Well, what we can do is buy a ticket for Khalid, leave him in the UK and then Yussuf can use the return portion.'

Again, Mahmoud considered it. 'I don't see how it can work. The airline will register that Khalid didn't check in, so how could he suddenly be coming back with you? And how are you going to get a stamp in his passport? If you fly to Beirut or Jordan, you still have to cross the border with Iraq, and there won't be a stamp in his passport to say that he entered Jordan.'

I hadn't thought of that.

'Well, I'll have to think of something, won't I?' I said tetchily. When Mahmoud played devil's advocate, he was generally right in his criticisms, and that was what I found irritating.

'And, anyway,' he went on, 'Yussuf doesn't look anything like Khalid. He's got black hair and dark eyes – Khalid is blond with green eyes. Any official will spot that.'

This was a big problem. We couldn't just dye Yussuf's hair blond – with Yussuf's dark skin colouring, our subterfuge would stand out a mile. I fell silent for a few minutes. Eventually, I worked out a plan.

'We'll shave his head,' I said. 'If I have any trouble at all with Customs, I'll tell them he had cancer and is having chemotherapy. It won't matter about the colour of his eyes – I'll give him a Valium before we get to the airport so he sleeps all the way through it. That should get their sympathy, and avoid them asking too many awkward questions.'

Mahmoud, as ever, was sceptical, but I was determined. Besides, I liked the idea of a trip to Iraq. I had decided to take Amira with me to meet her father's family. It would be an experience for her, and Mahmoud's mother would be over the moon to see her granddaughter. I had found a friend, Jane, who was willing to travel with us to help out. I was glad about that since travelling with two small children is a handful at the best of times; travelling illegally with one of them sedated could have proved too much for me.

We needed to get visas for both Jordan, where we would be heading initially, and, of course, Iraq. As Mahmoud's family are Iraqi, it was perfectly understandable that I would be taking the children to visit their relatives. Once the paperwork was sorted out, it was time to go. We headed off to Heathrow, a route which was becoming a well-trodden path.

The plan was for Mahmoud and Khalid to pretend they were coming with us. After checking in, I would claim that Khalid had become ill and was unable to fly. I would have to worry about how I was going to get a stamp for his passport when I got to Jordan.

As we checked in, though, I got a very lucky break. Khalid, whose health is frail anyway, complained that he wasn't feeling good. I felt his forehead and, sure enough, he was burning up. I made sure that the staff could hear me as I comforted him, and in a loud voice told him that he would have to go home with Daddy and join us in Iraq in a few days' time when his father flew out to meet us.

Of course, Mahmoud wasn't coming; I just wanted a plausible story as to why we wanted to keep the return portion of his flight. The man at the desk seemed slightly unsure as to whether this was acceptable, but with a long line of passengers to process for the flight, he let it go. We had got over the first hurdle.

We kissed Mahmoud and Khalid goodbye. I wouldn't be seeing them for a couple of weeks and, like many mums, I felt a pang of guilt at leaving my little boy, but Mahmoud reassured me that he would be fine. He was a good father and, I have to say, had always proved to be a supportive husband, especially given my many escapades, which many other husbands would not have been too happy about. We went through to the departures lounge and headed on to the plane.

It's not too long a flight to Amman, Jordan's capital city, and Amira managed to sleep the whole way. I was too anxious to rest, though, what with worrying over the conundrum of how to get a stamp for Khalid's passport. I went over and over it in my mind, but I couldn't think of a way around it. At last, I had to accept that there was no obvious solution and put my faith in God to present an answer.

When we landed, Jane could see that I was stressed and took Amira off my hands for a few minutes. As we headed into the airport terminal, we joined the queue at passport control. Up ahead, sitting at a high desk, was a man who was glancing at each passport before giving it a stamp. An idea had presented itself to me, but it was a risky one.

When we got near to the front of the queue, I began to call out loudly, 'Khalid, Khalid, come back here!'

With Amira in my free arm and the passports in the other, I hoped I was doing a passable impression of a harassed and fed-up mother. I stepped forward and handed the passports to the official. He asked where my son was, and I told him in Arabic that the naughty child had run on ahead and that I would be giving him a good talking to. I asked whether someone should go through and find him, but he smiled politely and said it wouldn't be necessary, whilst issuing the requisite stamps. He was obviously a man with small children of his own. I could have kissed him. That had been the thing that had worried me the most, the biggest flaw in my plan. We now had paperwork to show that Khalid was legally in the country, with a valid flight and visa. When we turned up with Yussuf, at least the paperwork would be in order, although, admittedly, we would have other things to worry about.

We collected our luggage and headed out of the terminal. Jane was heading to Lebanon, but would meet us again in Amman when we were coming back through, and return to London with us. I said goodbye, then, as usual, made my way to a group of drivers to haggle over the price of taking Amira and me to the Iraqi border, a considerable journey that would take many hours.

I agreed on a deal with one of them and we set off. It was a long, gruelling drive with little in the way of scenery to relieve the monotony. We drove through the north Jordanian desert, stopping every so often at roadside stalls to get a cold drink and something to eat. It was hot and dusty, and the car naturally had no air conditioning. To her credit, little Amira was very well-behaved and didn't complain.

At last, we reached the border where Mahmoud's mother, Fatima, was waiting for us with a car. We transferred our luggage from one car to the other, then set off again – we still had a long drive ahead of us before we reached Najaf. Mahmoud's father was a businessman so the family is relatively well off, by local standards anyway. They live in a large two-storey house with a big front garden that has fruit trees which offer shade from the sun. When we finally arrived, I was shattered, but glad to be there. If I thought I could go straight to bed, though, I was mistaken. Fatima had arranged a big welcoming meal with lots of relatives, all of whom were excitedly waiting to see little Amira. Sleep was going to have wait a little longer.

I rang Mahmoud to tell him we had arrived safely. I got to speak to Marlon and my little angel Khalid, who sounded much better than when I had last seen him 24 hours previously at Heathrow Airport. That was a big weight off my mind. We finally did get to go to bed, but not until we'd eaten a huge meal and endured hours of relatives cooing over pretty little Amira.

The next two weeks were going to be busy. Yussuf didn't speak a word of English, and we needed to do something about that. Although I was planning to sedate him so we could get past the officials at the airport, I couldn't run the risk of him waking up and starting to speak Arabic. That would have given the game away, as he was meant to be British.

I set about teaching Yussuf a few key words and phrases. It was imperative that he learned to call me Mummy, so I insisted that he refer to me like that from day one. I taught him the words for essentials like 'toilet' and 'water', and prayed that this smattering would be enough to get us through. I also took out some time to see a bit of Iraq. We visited some of the holy shrines and the countryside nearby, and went to visit Mahmoud's father's grave to pay our respects. I saw a lot of poverty in my short time there.

Being August, the heat was unbearable during the day, so trips had to be made first thing in the morning or early evening. The electricity supply was temperamental, coming on only for a few hours each day, so air conditioning was out of the question. I was thankful for the shade of the fruit trees in the garden on many occasions, and we spent a lot of time sitting around fanning ourselves.

Just like when I had lived with Karim's family in Jordan, I found myself very attracted to this simple, ancient way of life which had surely changed little since the days when the Koran was written. Despite the shortages, people seemed content and neighbourly, qualities sadly all too absent in the bustling communities of central London. I also loved the emphasis that Arabic cultures place upon the family unit. Everything revolved around it: relatives were always dropping in and, during my stay, there were many meals to which members of the extended family were invited.

But the time flew by all too quickly. Soon we had to put our audacious – some might say foolhardy – attempt to return to the UK into action, with Yussuf masquerading as Khalid. Yussuf's father had managed to obtain a visa for Jordan, which meant that he could accompany us on the first leg of the journey. Saying goodbye to Fatima was tough. She had been so happy to have Amira around for a couple of weeks that I knew it was very hard for her to say goodbye, knowing that we were heading to another world thousands of miles away. We didn't know when we would see her again – in fact, the next time we met things would be far less amicable and loving.

Back then, though, I had no inkling of what was to come. We made our way back to Jordan without mishap, although it naturally meant another gruelling journey through the desert, and the next day we arrived in Amman. Yussef said goodbye to his dad and we set to work. We had a while before we were due to fly back home, and we needed the time to make sure that Yussuf looked the part for the charade we had planned. We were staying at the apartment of a friend in Amman, and our first job was somehow to make Yussuf look like a child with leukaemia who was undergoing chemotherapy. No easy task.

The first thing we did was shave off his lovely head of dark hair. Khalid's passport described him as blond, so we had to shave him so closely that he was bald – even a fine covering of dark stubble would have given the game away. The poor kid was horrified at what we were doing to him and even my attempted jollity could not prevent tears welling up in his eyes. Next, I tackled his eyebrows and finally the light fuzz on his arms. We couldn't afford to take any risks.

Jane was flying from Beirut to meet us at the apartment, and she duly arrived that evening. Our flight was leaving at two in the morning, and we wanted to time our movements precisely since we were going to sedate Yussuf. We didn't want him to wake up at the wrong moment. We put a baseball cap on his head, and I dressed him in some of Khalid's Western-style clothes – jeans and a T-shirt. Even I had to admit he looked perfect.

Before we left the apartment to head for the airport, I gave Yussuf two Valium tablets with a glass of milk. He took them without complaint. By the time the taxi dropped us off at the airport, he was fast asleep. So far, so good. We checked in for the flight and headed towards the departures lounge. As we approached the passport desk, my stomach was churning with fear and my mouth was as dry as blotting paper. Although I had done this same thing many times, this was the first time I had attempted to undertake a rescue on my own with false papers. I was only too aware that, if anything went wrong, I would be certain to end up in prison. I began to panic that maybe I had bitten off more than I could chew.

I approached the desk, hoping that my fear wasn't showing on my face, and handed over our passports. The official took them from me and seemed to take a few seconds to study my face before he opened the passports. He took his time studying them, before glancing back at me with what looked like suspicion etched on his face. Finally, he spoke. Nodding towards Yussuf, he said, 'Your son. Why did he not go to Iraq with you?'

I felt sick with fear. He had spotted that Amira and I had stamps showing that we had crossed into Iraq, but, of course, Khalid's passport didn't have any. I decided the only way through this was to brazen it out. Gesturing towards Yussuf, I said, 'Can't you see how sick my son is? He is dying of cancer. We wanted to take him to Iraq to see his family and to take him to a shrine before he died, but he was too ill to make the journey. We had to leave him here in Amman with friends and go without him.'

The official looked at me a little longer. He didn't seem entirely convinced by my explanation, but maybe it was my paranoia that was making me feel that way. Eventually, he nodded, shut the passports and handed them back.

'OK, Madam,' he said. 'Have a pleasant flight.'

We were through! Jane followed us, and we found somewhere to sit and let my beating heart calm down. I didn't look back, convinced that the official was watching me, looking for any sign of suspicious behaviour. Just then, an announcement came over the Tannoy, informing us that our flight had been delayed by three hours. This was disastrous. All our plans had been made on the tightest possible timings. The airport officials already seemed suspicious of us and hanging around the terminal with a drugged child could only serve to draw further, unwelcome attention to ourselves.

We had only been sitting for a few minutes when Yussuf began to come round and started mumbling.

'Shit,' said Jane. 'What are we going to do now?'

'We don't have any choice,' I said firmly. 'We'll have to give him another Valium.'

Jane was dubious. She was worried that he might have a

reaction, that we might be unconsciously giving him an overdose, but I was sure we were still within safe limits. He mumbled again. I leaned down to see what he wanted. He was saying he wanted to go to the toilet.

We had taken the precaution of putting a nappy on him in case he needed the toilet while he was sedated, and Jane suggested letting him go in the nappy, but I thought it was a bad idea. For one thing, it would have been very unpleasant for Yussuf, and if he had got upset, he might have started crying and attracting other people's attention. For another, we might need to rely on the nappy later for a real emergency, perhaps when we were on the plane and he was out for the count. Reluctantly, Jane accepted these points and agreed to take him to the toilet.

While they were gone, I sat with Amira, who was wide awake and in need of some stimulation and attention. As we played, to my horror, I heard my name being called out, requesting that I return to passport control. Oh, my God! Had we been rumbled? The official must have decided that he wanted a second look at our papers. My legs almost turned to jelly as I stood up.

I carried Amira back down the escalator and towards where we had come from. I felt sick and was convinced that I had been caught. There was no way out of my predicament; there is nowhere to hide in an airport and there would be no way of getting into the aeroplane. My best bet was to be cooperative and polite, and throw myself on the mercy of the courts. Perhaps they would understand that I was just trying to help reunite a mother and son, and would be lenient with me. In my heart, though, I didn't really believe it. Travelling on false papers is a serious offence, and I didn't think the courts would view it as a trivial matter. I became convinced that I was likely to end up in prison and could only think about my darling children. How had I allowed myself to end up in such a crazy situation?

I approached passport control. The suspicious official who had checked my papers earlier had now been joined by a couple of colleagues, who were probably there to provide back-up in case I became hysterical. No doubt the police would be there in a few minutes. As I approached the desk, certain I was walking towards the inevitable loss of my freedom, I resolved to keep my head held high.

What I had done was not a bad thing, I told myself. I was proud of my work helping to reunite mothers and children in the past, and if I were to go to prison for it, so be it. There would surely be an international outcry, and the story would certainly make the news back home. At least it would raise public awareness of the lack of protection mothers have within the law and that the Hague Convention had been ignored by countries in the Middle East. It might illustrate why mothers were forced to resort to measures that were supposedly illegal, and why the equivalent acts of fathers who had abducted the children in the first place were ignored.

I had worked myself up into such a lather of righteous indignation that by the time I reached the desk I was ready to give these officials a piece of my mind. I had even forgotten that we were there not to rescue a child, but to bring one home to my sister-in-law!

The wind was taken out of my sails when one of them simply said, 'May we take another look at your papers, Madam?'

I fished my passport out of my handbag and handed it over, wondering what was going on. The official took a look at the pages of stamps inside, then said, 'I am afraid your visa expired three days ago. There is a small sum to be paid.'

I almost burst out laughing with sheer relief, but managed to restrain myself. One minute I was convinced I was about to be carted away to some hellish Arabic prison, my head filled with scenes from the film *Midnight Express*; the next, I was being told that there had been a slight infringement of minor local rules, and I needed to pay a few pounds to settle the matter. I handed over the money, and the official smiled politely as he handed back my passport.

'Thank you, Madam,' he said. 'Have a safe trip.'

I went back up to where I had last seen Jane and Yussuf, trying not to let myself grin too broadly, though I desperately wanted to. They were back from the toilet, and when I told Jane what I had just been through, we couldn't help but giggle, keeping our voices low so as not to draw undue attention to ourselves.

At last, it was time to board our plane. We headed out through departures onto the tarmac. My nerves were so frayed by this stage that I could hardly even bear to look the airline staff in the eye as they smiled and welcomed us aboard. The sight of anyone in uniform was making me twitchy now. Yussuf was fast asleep again, having had a third Valium inside the terminal, and I hoped that the sight of a mother with her tragically ill little boy would elicit some sympathy and ensure that we were given space.

It seemed to work. We were on board and seated without any problems. I wouldn't be able to relax until we were airborne, though – and even then I knew we would still have to negotiate our stopover in Athens, in Greece, and, after that, Immigration in Heathrow, possibly the greatest test of all.

We needn't have worried about officialdom in Athens. As soon as the plane had landed, we were being rushed down the stairs and across to another plane that would be taking us for the next leg of the journey back to London. We hardly had time to feel the balmy heat of the Greek afternoon before we were loaded up and taking off.

On the plane, I discussed with Jane what we should do. Passport control at Heathrow was tough, far tougher than in Amman. There, they are presumably less worried about who is leaving the country than they are at Heathrow about who is arriving. We had no option but to see our plan through. We had checked Yussuf in at Amman on Khalid's passport, so we would have to carry on at Heathrow. We just had to hope that a mother with two small children might seem less suspicious, and that they would not examine anything too closely.

Jane squeezed my hand. 'We've made it this far,' she reassured me. 'Don't lose your faith.'

I smiled. Having a friend alongside me was immensely comforting. I am certain that I could not have done this on my own. My nerve would have failed at Amman Airport and I would probably have turned myself in long before now.

Heathrow was reassuringly grey, as it always seems to be. I hoped that this would be an omen that normal service was being resumed, that we would have no problems. We joined the line of people queuing at passport control. I was carrying Yussuf, who had his baseball cap pulled down. He really didn't look too good, what with the effects of the Valium, the shearing job I had done on him and the gruelling effect of the long journey. After all, it had been nearly 48 hours since we had left Najaf. I was shattered, never mind a six-year-old boy who had never left home before and who had been on an aeroplane for the first time in his life.

The officials were brisk and efficient, nodding us through after glancing at our papers. Had we made it? We still had to get our luggage and clear Customs.

Yussuf, who was awake but groggy, started to whinge. He was speaking in Arabic, and getting louder and louder, so that people were beginning to look at us. I was so tired that my brain wasn't functioning and I couldn't seem to understand what he was saying. My foggy mind managed to pick out the words for toilet, so I left Jane by the carousel waiting for our bags, while I took Yussuf to the bathrooms.

When we came back out, there was a man in a suit with a badge that identified him as 'security'. He was flanked by two chaps in uniform, and they were clearly waiting for me. What was wrong? Had Yussuf speaking Arabic given the game away?

'Is everything OK, Madam?' he asked, walkie-talkie in hand.

In for a penny, in for a pound, I told myself, taking a deep breath. I did my best imitation of a woman at the end of her tether – to tell the truth, I didn't need to act too much. I told him that my son had cancer, that we'd had a long and exhausting flight and, to cap it all, our bags still had not appeared.

He apologised and explained that bags were slow to appear on the carousel as a number of baggage handlers were off – I can't remember if he said they were sick, on strike or had turned into fairies, I was so nervous. He asked me to describe our bags and said that he would arrange someone to collect them for us. In the mean time, we could sit down and take the weight off our feet.

A few minutes later, he reappeared with our luggage piled on a trolley. We thanked him for his kindness. People complain about British service, but when you have travelled as much as I have, you begin to appreciate that people here in the UK really are far more polite and helpful than they get credit for. We're always very keen to run our own country down, but let me tell you, after the anarchy and chaos of some of the countries that I have visited, I have sometimes felt like kneeling down on the runway and kissing the tarmac, like the Pope, when I get back to Heathrow.

We wheeled our trolley through Customs and out into the main terminal building. There, on the other side of the barrier, was Mahmoud, my rock. We had made it; and I will never forget the emotional scenes later that day when Ibtihal and Yussuf were reunited.

For all the scares, the anxiety, the fear of imprisonment, I wouldn't have changed what I was doing for all the tea in China. Seeing the look on these mothers' faces when they get their children back was the most rewarding pay I could have had.

Chapter 7

My Wings Clipped

When I had first started helping mothers, I was very careful not to let word spread too widely about the missions I was undertaking. Not only were they illegal and could have resulted in trouble for me with the authorities, I was also conscious that many within the community would not take a favourable view of them. I didn't want my children to have any stigma attached to them, or to be given a hard time at school by the children of parents who disapproved of what I was doing. Still, I was always pleasantly surprised by the reaction of most people around me.

On top of this, I had begun to be contacted by journalists. People probably don't realise just how persistent the media can be, how skilled they are in tracking you down. They are able to pay money for stories and for information; many people are swayed by that and are willing to pass on details. That must be how they tracked me down. The first few times it happened, I was absolutely horrified and hung up, but little by little, the journalists who rang reassured me that my name would be changed in the articles they wrote, and that there would be nothing in them to identify me or my children. So articles began to appear, and the world didn't cave in.

The next stage was that television companies got in touch, saying they would like me to appear on their shows to discuss the problem of child abduction. I agreed to appear on a couple of them, namely daytime-TV staples *Trisha* and *GMTV*, and made sure that I was well-disguised with my headscarf. I also insisted that they only referred to me as Dee. I felt that it was a good thing to publicise the fact that these things did happen. It was as though child abduction was the skeleton in the cupboard of British Islam, and I wanted to ensure that as many people knew about it as possible, at least so that other vulnerable mothers could learn to be on their guard against it.

One effect of having a public profile was that I began to be contacted by members of the public, who would send letters to the television production companies. They would in turn pass them on to me. In 99 per cent of cases, these letters were supportive and invariably from women who were in the same predicament, begging me to help them – it was very rare that anyone criticised me or what I was doing to help mothers. One of the correspondence letters was an email from a lady called Sarra Fotheringham. I recalled having seen her on the *Tonight with Trevor McDonald* programme. Her son was being held in Dubai, and she could not see him. Something about her letter touched me, and I decided to ring her. We spoke on the phone and agreed to meet up at the office – Café Rouge in Whiteleys, in case anyone needs reminding.

I made my way down on the agreed day, and Sarra came up and introduced herself. I suppose she recognised me from seeing me on television. She was in her mid-30s, attractive and with a good figure. Her blonde hair was pulled back into a ponytail, and she was fashionably dressed in jeans and cowboy boots. She was well-spoken, although her accent seemed ever so slightly affected, as though she'd worked hard on it, and she wore slightly too much make-up for my tastes. Still, one should not judge a person by their appearance, and I sat back and waited to hear what she had to say.

Sarra lived in Camberley, a commuter town in Surrey, with her husband Neil, a policeman, and their three children. Many years earlier, she had worked as an air hostess for the UAE-based airline Emirates, which meant she spent a lot of time in Dubai. Being a keen horse rider, she had used stables in Dubai, which happened to be near to the Metropolitan Hotel. During one of these visits, she met a handsome, charming young man called Rashid Al Habtoor, who kept his polo ponies there. Polo is a sport enjoyed by the very wealthy in Dubai, as it is in most countries, so he was obviously well-connected. Just how well-connected, Sarra would find out much later. Indeed, his family owned both the hotel and the stables.

Like many wealthy, Western-educated Arab men, Rashid seemed very attracted to well-presented Western women, and with her shapely figure and blonde hair, Sarra was no exception. They got chatting and Rashid invited her out to dinner. They began to have an affair, and Sarra, only 23 at the time, soon fell for this rich, handsome, urbane man. When she realised she was pregnant, she discovered a side to Rashid she had not glimpsed until then. He grew cold, and said he wanted nothing to do with her or the baby, not an unusual reaction from these playboys of the Eastern world. Saddened and a little wiser, Sarra returned to the UK and had the child, a son whom she named Tariq in tribute to his Arabic blood.

She sent a letter to Rashid, informing him that he had a son, but never received a reply. Like many wealthy Arab men who have flings with Western women, he was almost certainly suspicious, believing it to be a trap to get at his wealth. Later, Sarra heard that he had married an Arab woman, and she set about bringing up Tariq as a single mother.

Within a few years, when Tariq was four, Sarra met Neil and, in due course, they got married. Sarra explained that it was a relief to meet a man who was prepared to look on her first-born as his own. I nodded sympathetically. It had been the same for me when I had married Mahmoud and saw how good he was with Marlon, my first son. Indeed, Neil went so far as to officially adopt Tariq and they had him christened. Sarra and Neil then had a further three children in quick succession.

When Tariq – or TT, as Sarra called him – was seven, she determined to get in touch with Rashid once again, believing that, as the boy grew older, he would want to get to know his natural father. With his darker skin and black hair, it was obvious that he had a different father to his three siblings, so opening lines of communication now would surely bear fruit in the long run.

To her surprise, Rashid wrote back this time. He said that he would want a paternity test to prove beyond doubt that he was Tariq's father. Many wealthy men are convinced that the world is full of women out to bring paternity suits against them in an effort to get their hands on their wealth – it even happened to the actress and model Liz Hurley when she had a son by the American billionaire Steve Bing. If these men can't trust a rich woman like Liz Hurley, it shows how suspicious they can be. Sarra was insulted, but decided to do it to settle the matter.

Of course, the tests came back positive, and suddenly there was a great change in Rashid's attitude. By this stage, he had children of his own, so perhaps that made him take his responsibilities as a father more seriously. He came to the UK a few times to see the Fotheringhams and meet his son, and then he made the whole family an offer. He would pay for them all to go out to Dubai, he would provide them with a house where they could live, and pay for all of the children to be educated, not just Tariq. The only problem was what Neil would do for a living. Rashid had even thought of that. They would employ him as a fitness instructor in one of the hotels they owned. They discussed the offer and decided that they would give it a go.

At first, the expat life suited them. Dubai is an opulent place, and there is a good life to be had for those that can afford it. Nevertheless, after a while, the Fotheringhams grew tired of the lifestyle in this sunshine state and began to long for home. There was a litany of problems, Sarra said: the house was too small for them, they hardly got to see TT, who spent most of his free time at his father's, and Neil was not enjoying his new job. After several months out in Dubai, they resolved to return home. She told Rashid of their decision. He told them that it was their decision, but if they did go home, it would be without TT. Sarra couldn't believe what she was hearing.

Believing the law to be on her side, she went to the British Embassy to enlist their help. Then came the body blow. 'They told us there was nothing they could do,' Sarra said, her eyes welling up with tears at the injustice of it all. 'As TT had gone of his own free will to Dubai, Rashid wasn't breaking any laws. They said that the courts would uphold a father's right to be with his son. It was so unfair.'

Heartbroken, they returned to the UK and began mounting a legal bid. They were initially buoyed to win a case in the High Court, ruling that they should have custody, but Rashid appealed, and the Appeal Court ruled that the courts in Dubai had jurisdiction. As an adoptive father, Neil had no rights – Dubai does not recognise adoption as legally binding.

By now, Sarra had found out how powerful the Al Habtoors were. Rashid was chairman of his family's holding company and was a very powerful man. He was reputed to have played polo with Prince Charles, and counted people like Prince Michael of Kent and Omar Sharif among his friends and acquaintances. The trading company his family owned was a powerful conglomerate, with hotel, publishing, engineering and property interests. They were also very close to the Al Maktoums, the ruling family of Abu Dhabi. Sarra couldn't have picked a more powerful enemy if she had tried.

It was hopeless. No court in Dubai was going to award her custody of Tariq against such a family. She cried as she told me that she had been limited to one phone call a week and that she feared if she didn't act soon, she would lose TT forever as he adopted the Muslim faith and Arabic culture.

I asked her what TT felt about the situation, and she told me that every time she rang, he was in tears, asking her when he could come home. I sympathised. I had seen this sort of thing all too often, and I knew how it tore families apart. I was determined to help this poor woman in any way I could.

One thing that worried me was that, in his emails to his mother, TT talked about a man named Adel, who had been hired as a bodyguard specifically to protect him from an attempted snatching. We would have to plan very carefully.

I pored over maps of the region to work out how we could do it. Assuming we managed to reach TT – a big assumption, given the bodyguard – our best route would be to get to Port Rashid in Dubai and take a boat from there to Umm Qasr, a port in Iraq. I would travel alone with the boy, using Marlon's passport for him, and arrange for a contact to meet us in Umm Qasr. By travelling with him, we would look like a normal family and attract less suspicion. We could then cross Iraq and make our way into Jordan, flying home from Amman – a route with which I was very familiar.

There were two advantages to this plan. The Al Habtoors would be expecting us to fly out of the country, so would arrange for the airports to be watched. I doubted that it would occur to such a wealthy family that anyone would use such a common form of transport as a ferry. The other advantage was that if they watched Sarra, she would act as a decoy and draw them away from what we were doing.

I explained the plan to Sarra and Neil, and they seemed happy. Or rather Sarra seemed happy. Neil didn't strike me as that smart for someone who was supposed to have been a policeman. I couldn't picture him stopping someone for speeding, let alone helping to rescue this child. He seemed to go along with whatever Sarra had decided.

In February 2002, we were ready to make a move. Neil drove us both to Heathrow, and we took a plane to Abu Dhabi. If the Al Habtoors were as powerful as I was beginning to realise they were, it was entirely possible that they had people checking passenger lists into Dubai for Sarra's name. If they were alerted to the fact that we were in the country, our mission would be scuppered before we'd even begun.

We hired a car in Abu Dhabi and drove north to Dubai. We checked into the Hilton under false names and hatched our plans. I explained to Sarra that we would start by using the same methods as I had employed on previous undercover missions: we would stake out the house where TT was staying and try to get a feel for what the daily routine was. We would do this for a few days and look for the best moment to carry out our plan.

The next day, Sarra drove me to the large, comfortable house where TT was living with his father. Across the road was a far more opulent mansion. 'That's where Rashid's father lives,' Sarra told me. It was clear that the Al Habtoors were wealthy and a couple of days' surveillance bore out this observation. An army of servants – drivers, maids, God knows what – came and went, but we could never see any sign of TT. Security appeared to be good. We needed to try to find another chink in their armour.

We knew that TT went to the Emirates International School, so we would have to see whether we had any chance of picking him up from there.

'We'll head down there,' I said. 'You stay in the car, and I'll go in, pretend that I've just moved to Dubai and am interested in enrolling my son at the school. That way I can see the lie of the land.'

Sarra didn't look convinced, but I reassured her, saying, 'Don't worry, I've done this lots of times. It'll be fine.'

The next morning, we drove down to the school and Sarra parked a short distance away. I headed in, noting the presence of guards on the gates, and was shown to the school office. I explained that I had just moved to Dubai from Jordan and was looking for a school for my son who was 11. Could I be shown around? Of course, it was no problem – they even showed me the class he would be joining. I looked around the room, sure that Tariq must be in there, but I couldn't pick him out from all the faces. They all looked similar, with the same hair and colouring.

I thanked them for their time, and they showed me out of the school. Apart from the guards on the gates, the security seemed lax. This would be the best place to make our attempt. I told Sarra, and we agreed to come back the next day and try to carry out the 'rescue'.

When we came back the following day, we made sure that we arrived in good time, before all the children. We drove straight into the school, since everyone else seemed to arrive by car; it would be a way of drawing the least amount of attention to ourselves. As the children began to arrive, we scoured the sea of faces, looking out for Tariq. We were dressed traditionally, with full veils, so we didn't stand out. It was getting close to the time for the start of school, and there was still no sign of him. We even darted into the school and made our way to the classroom that had been pointed out to me, but there were few children there, and no Tariq.

By now, we were getting desperate. We headed back out to the playground. This area was arranged according to year, so we found the section for Tariq's year. Leaning against a fence was a muscular man, 6 ft 6 in. tall, wearing a leather jacket and smoking a cigarette.

'That must be Adel, the bodyguard,' I whispered to Sarra. 'We need to be quick. Is there any sign of him?'

'I can't see him!' she whispered back, eyes darting around above her veil as she scanned the sea of faces in the playground. Luckily for us, the bodyguard didn't appear to be paying much attention, enjoying a crafty cigarette while he could. It probably didn't occur to him that anyone would try to snatch the child from right under his nose, inside a school with guards at the front gate.

Suddenly Sarra stiffened. 'There he is,' she hissed, gesturing towards a group of boys on the far side of the playground.

I looked over at the bodyguard, and, fortunately, he was still engrossed in his own private world. When I looked back, Sarra had already rushed over to the boys and was bending down to one of them, the one that must have been Tariq. But the whole thing seemed slightly odd. From what I'd seen on previous trips, as soon as children recognised their mother, they'd fling their arms around them and the two would stand rooted to the spot, not letting go of each other until I was forced to remind them that we had to move. This time, Tariq didn't seem to be reacting. I went over to them, and Sarra was trying to reason with him. She was telling him that he needed to come with her, but he was refusing.

'I mustn't, Mummy, Daddy told me I'm not allowed to.'

Sarra scoffed, telling him that she was his mother, and he could go wherever she said he could go.

He didn't move and said, 'But I'm not allowed to go anywhere without Adel,' looking over nervously to where the bodyguard was still failing to look in our direction. We had two minutes before the bell would ring and the playground would empty out, leaving us horribly exposed.

'Sarra,' I hissed. 'We need to get in the car now.' We each took an arm and hurried Tariq towards the car. As he seemed to be resisting, we ended up practically carrying him and bundled him into the back seat, before jumping in ourselves. Sarra put the car in gear and began to head towards the gates. Unfortunately, all the other cars were trying to leave at the same time, so we had to join a queue, inching forwards to get out. I was holding my breath, expecting an alarm to go off any second and the bodyguard to come running over to us. As we went through, I pulled Tariq down and covered him up with a top that was lying on the back seat.

The guards hardly glanced at us, and we pulled out onto the main road. We had made it!

Once we had got away from the school, we could relax a little and I began to take stock of our situation. Tariq was very unhappy, saying that he had to go back. Sarra dismissed his objections, telling him that he would be coming back to England with her, and how nice it would be for him to see his granddad and the other children, but it didn't seem to allay his worries. He looked frightened and uncomfortable at being in the car with us.

Sarra handed me her mobile and asked me to phone her father's number.

'Here, TT,' she said brightly, 'why don't you have a word with Granddad? He'd love to hear from you . . .'

Tariq had a short conversation, but in all honesty it didn't seem to cheer him up a great deal. He sat in the back seat sulking, then demanded his Game Boy, which Sarra had brought with her to comfort him. He soon became engrossed with that, which gave us time to think.

By now, I was feeling very uncomfortable with what we had done. Usually, when I carried out a rescue, a child would be so delighted to see its mother, there was no questioning. The child would simply leap into his or her mother's arms, and do whatever it was told without question. I had been taken aback by the lack of warmth between Sarra and Tariq. Far from being so miserable in Dubai, as Sarra had led me to believe, the opposite seemed to be the case with Tariq. He was unhappy at being taken out of school and away from his bodyguard, and seemed very worried about what his dad would say.

And the fact that we'd had to practically manhandle him into the car was troubling. It felt as though we were taking him against his will. Occasionally, newspapers had described me as a 'professional kidnapper', something with which I always took issue. I believe myself to be someone who rescues abducted children and reunites them with their mothers when they have been taken away against their will. What we had just done felt more akin to a kidnapping, though, and it made me uneasy.

It was far too late to be having those sort of doubts now, though. We had a child in the back of the car, and there was no doubt that the authorities here would view it as a straight kidnapping, particularly given the power and influence of the Al Habtoor family. The ferry to Iraq from Port Rashid wasn't due to sail until that afternoon, and I was becoming nervous at having to wait that long – particularly if the alarm had gone up and the authorities were beginning to look for us.

I rang Mahmoud for some advice. 'I don't think we should hang around waiting for the ferry,' I told him. 'I'm thinking we might be better off driving to Qatar and into Iraq that way. At least it means we'll still be on the move.'

Mahmoud pointed out that to get to Qatar we would first have to cross into Saudi Arabia. It felt dangerous, changing our plans so suddenly and so rashly, but I couldn't see how we could hang around Port Rashid for several hours with a reluctant child and not draw attention to ourselves. It felt like too great a risk.

I told Sarra what I was thinking, and we agreed to drive to Iraq along the coastal route through Qatar. At least we would be on the move and doing something. We headed back to the Hilton, where we got our luggage and paid our bill, before we got back on the desert highway heading for the Saudi border. Tariq had fallen silent now, playing with his Game Boy or staring out the window. Something didn't feel at all right.

We stopped for a toilet break just before border control. I could see a lorry driver sitting in the shade having a rest, so I went up to him and started a conversation as casually as I could. 'Hello,' I said in Arabic. 'How long will it take us to get to Qatar from here?'

The driver glanced over at the car, where Sarra was stretching her legs. Seeing no one else around, he looked surprised and asked, 'Where's your driver?'

I laughed, like an idiot, and said, 'That's her right there.'

He shook his head, as though he was talking to a fool – which, with hindsight, he was. 'Women can't drive in Saudi. You'll be pulled over. Have you got visas for Qatar?'

Of course we didn't. Qatar hadn't been part of our plans, so we didn't have the necessary paperwork. I told him as much, hoping against hope that this stranger could come up with a plan that could save our bacon. But, of course, he couldn't. He shook his head once more. 'Well, if you don't have papers for Qatar, you're stuck. Even if you could pay someone to drive your car across Saudi for you, you'd just be turned back at the next border.' He looked away, returning to his cigarette, no doubt thinking how silly we were.

I went back to the car to break the bad news to Sarra.

'Well, then,' she trilled, 'we'll just have to go back to Port Rashid and stick to the original plan.' I couldn't tell if she really did have no idea of the gravity of our situation, or if she was simply one of life's optimists, determined to make the best of a bad job. I suspected it was a little bit of both.

We drove back through the Abu Dhabi desert to Dubai and Port Rashid. When we got to the port, I was looking to see if there was anything out of the ordinary, such as roadblocks or obvious police activity, but I couldn't see anything. Perhaps we were going to be OK. For all we knew, alarm bells weren't ringing yet; the school may have just thought that Tariq was off sick. Maybe they wouldn't discover he had gone until the end of the school day when Adel, the bodyguard, was sent to collect him. I cheered up a little. All was not lost.

I got Sarra to drive down by the docks to the ticket office. The ferry was due to sail in less than an hour, so at least we wouldn't have to hang around for too long. I got out of the car and told Sarra to drive around the block and come back for me in ten minutes. I went in and bought two first-class tickets for the ferry – I didn't want Tariq to be complaining about the conditions on board. Something told me that he wasn't accustomed to travelling economy.

With the tickets in my handbag, I went back outside and waited by the road. I could see Sarra coming, and she pulled up beside me. As I opened the back door and went to get in the back of the car, I felt a hand on my shoulder. I turned around and there was a group of men in traditional Arab dress. One of them produced some papers, showing that they were undercover police, and said that we were under arrest.

This was it! I had finally been caught. In all the missions I had undertaken, my luck had finally run out. I was really scared. All my misgivings about what we were doing flooded into my mind. The fact that Tariq had been so reluctant to come with us made it inevitable that we would be charged with kidnapping. Any clemency that a court might show to a misguided but essentially loving mother would not apply in this case. We had taken a child from under the nose of his bodyguard, despite the child begging us not to do it and asking to be returned to his father.

Grim-faced, the police escorted us into a police building within the port. Inside, it was pandemonium. We were taken to a room, and told to sit and wait. The uniformed police at the station were kind to us, offering us tea, but the undercover guys who had arrested us were utterly humourless and stony-faced. Things were looking bad. I had been allowed to take my shoulder bag from the car, and it was a small mercy that they hadn't searched it. Inside, were all our maps and escape routes, which would show that we had planned this whole operation and could be charged with conspiracy, as well as attempted kidnapping – although the latter was bad enough.

It became clear that we were waiting for someone, though they wouldn't tell us who. We soon found out – Rashid Al Habtoor and his father. Both were dressed in Arab robes and, from the deferential way the police treated them, I could tell they were every bit as powerful and influential as I had feared. Rashid wanted to take Tariq straight away, but the police officer in charge respectfully pointed out that the question of who had custody had to be settled first.

There had been the Court of Appeal decision which had stated that the Dubai courts had jurisdiction in this matter, while Sarra believed that she had custody. Because she had taken Tariq there legally and willingly, Dubai had become his habitual residence, and, naturally, Dubai law would side with Rashid. It wouldn't take long for them to ascertain that Rashid was the rightful father with custody.

In the mean time, though, we were taken in a convoy of police cars, sirens flashing, to the main police station elsewhere in the town. They took it in turns to question Sarra and me. In a brief, whispered exchange before we were separated, we agreed that our story should be that she had just come to Dubai to see her son, but at first sight had rashly and foolishly allowed her emotions to overcome her judgement, and grabbed him. This would make it an unplanned act of love, rather than a calculated plan.

The police were firm but fair. They allowed us to stop every so often for a break and a drink, and I have no complaints at all about the way we were treated. At one point when my interrogator left the room, I seized the opportunity to grab all the maps and paperwork from my bag and stuff them down the back of his desk to get rid of any incriminating evidence.

Eventually, after hours of questioning, the matter was decided. Tariq was free to return home with his father. For us, though, the picture was far bleaker. Sarra was to be charged with kidnapping. And I was charged with being an accessory to kidnapping.

I let out a little cry, and my eyes filled with tears. All my bravado had gone. How could I have been so stupid as to get involved in such a murky case? My tendency to jump in feet first had now got me in a world of trouble. Had I thought it through logically and carefully, this case was very different to ones I had worked on in the past. Usually, the father would have kidnapped the child I was trying to rescue from the UK. Two wrongs don't make a right, but it would have put me in a stronger position, had I been caught, if I could say that the father was a kidnapper, that he had committed a major crime in taking his child out of the UK and that there was a UK court ruling ordering that the child be returned to its mother.

This case was entirely different. Not only had the Fotheringhams taken Tariq to Dubai of their own free will, they had done so because there was a financial incentive for them to do so – the free house, the education, the job for Neil. Furthermore, the court ruling, both in the UK and Dubai, had been in Rashid's favour. We were completely outside the law. I felt alone and very frightened. When would I see my own darling children again?

We were led downstairs to the cells and checked in, and our possessions and jewellery were taken from us. The cell was spartan, as cells usually are, but at least it was clean. After a while, I was allowed out to use the phone. I rang home and told Mahmoud what had happened. His voice sounded sad and distant. I told him to look after the children for me and not to lose faith. Back in the cell, I lay down on the mattress and thought of the children. I should have been with them, cuddling them and watching over them as they went off to sleep. Instead, I was in a dirty cell thousands of miles away, in the biggest trouble that I had ever been in. I cried myself to sleep. It wouldn't be the last time.

The next day, we were moved to new cells. There was a whole bunch of women of various nationalities there, and a lot of Eastern Europeans who were in for prostitution. They were all very friendly, and it made me think that, much as we judge others from the safety of our comfortable lives, when the chips are down people are just people. I met an Englishwoman named Vicky Clarke who was in for something to do with drugs. She was lovely, and it was nice to have someone to talk to other than Sarra, who was beginning to annoy me. She kept saying stupid things, like how we would be out within hours once the British press got hold of this, and how Neil would sort everything out. She seemed to be living in some sort of fantasy world, completely in denial about what was happening to us.

Vicky explained that she was on remand, waiting to go up in front of the public prosecutor. She had been waiting for four months – I got the impression that in Dubai the wheels of justice turned very slowly. Vicky advised me on which public prosecutor to avoid, saying one of them was a real hang 'em and flog 'em sadist, if ever there was one. This was borne out by the few women listening who spoke English. They chipped in with anecdotes, agreeing with Vicky's assessment. This served to send me into a depression, as I wondered when I would get out. I really believed it could be years. At last it was lights out, and I thankfully fell into a deep sleep, no doubt from nervous exhaustion.

The next morning, Sarra was called upstairs to see someone from the British Embassy. She was gone for well over an hour, as I waited anxiously below. Would there be any good news? She came back down with a spring in her step, full of optimism. Despite the fact that she could be rather irritating, you couldn't help but admire her spirit.

Then it was my turn. I was shown to a meeting room and introduced to a woman called Suzanne. Also in the room was a big jolly man with a beard, who described himself as the head of human rights, whatever that meant. Suzanne asked if there was anything that I wanted and I asked for a few essentials, like toothpaste and a towel, and for her to let my family know I was OK.

She let me know that the case had been all over the papers back home, which wasn't a good thing. If Neil had been shooting his mouth off about how we had gone out to bring Tariq home, it would blow our story out of the water. Also, no country likes to be told what to do by another. I was afraid the Dubai authorities may have been provoked by negative press coverage into making an example of us.

It was explained to me that charges were almost inevitable and were likely to mean a sentence of three years. I felt myself crumple at this and, like a child, said, 'But Sarra said everything was going to be OK.'

Suzanne shook her head despairingly. 'I don't know what could have given her that idea. Some people will only hear what they want to hear.'

I thanked them for their time, and was taken back down.

Later that afternoon, we were on the move again. A big group of us were being taken to the main women's prison, a couple of hours' drive away, in a windowless van. I was relieved that Vicky was coming with us. The police, as ever, were very kind to us, telling us not to worry, that where we were going was a nice prison with a garden, and assuring us that we would be well looked after.

But when we got there, it looked like any prison – huge, forbidding and imposing. I felt my spirits being crushed. After being checked in, we were introduced to the woman who ran the prison, their equivalent of a governor. She was a sweet woman and said that she was sorry we were there, that she didn't think anyone should be locked up for trying to reunite a mother and a son, and I am certain that she meant it.

Sarra and I were put into a cell with Vicky and a Filipino woman. There were two bunks on each wall, but no blankets or pillows. The hardest part about being in prison was the sheer monotony. We stayed in our cells most of the day, with the odd change in routine when we were taken to the canteen to eat. This was a depressing experience. There was no natural light in the room and the food was muck, invariably some sort of stew. Even if I had wanted to eat, there was no cutlery, and I couldn't bring myself to scoop the filth up with my hands as some of the other women were doing.

I couldn't face using the toilets, which were filthy. I was worried that I might catch something from one of the prostitutes. We were allowed a shower once a day, though, and for that I was grateful. After a few days, Sarra and I were told we would be going up in front of the public prosecutor. We were handcuffed and put into another van. On the way to court, we stopped at the police station where we had first been taken, presumably to pick up more prisoners.

On a whim, I asked to see the jolly man with the beard, the head of human rights. To my surprise, they agreed. I was shown into his office, and he asked what he could do for me. I went into a litany of complaints about the prison where we were being held.

'It's a disgrace,' I said. 'These poor women have no blankets, no pillows, the food is inedible, there is no cutlery, the toilets are filthy . . . if that's not an infringement of their basic human rights, I don't know what is.'

I hadn't really expected any great response, but he smiled and said, 'Leave it with me. I'll see what I can do.' His kindness, and that of our police warders, served to lift my spirits, and I dared to believe that perhaps things wouldn't be so bad after all. After a few hours' driving, stopping every so often to get water, we arrived at the public prosecutor's office in Dubai. There was a lot of British media there, including staff from the *Tonight with Trevor McDonald* programme, who, of course, knew Sarra from her earlier appearance on the show. At least someone was taking an interest in our case, though that was no guarantee of special treatment. Sarra went in first and when she came out, I wasn't given the chance to speak to her. It was my turn.

I learned that I would be up in front of the chief prosecutor, the one about whom I had been warned. He didn't look so intimidating – he was a slight man with gold-rimmed glasses – but when he began to speak, I understood why everyone was so frightened of him. He literally shook with anger, asking how we could dare to come to his country and try to kidnap Tariq, tearing him away from his father. We had tried to make a mockery of his country's laws, laws that meant the smooth running of society and all that he represented, and for that we would pay. He set a date for our hearing and then agreed that we were free to go on bail, provided we surrendered our passports and did not try to leave Dubai.

He glared at me. 'Any attempt to leave the country, you will be back in jail – and next time you will not be coming out.'

There was just one snag – as well as surrendering our passports, someone had to stand surety for us by surrendering theirs.

'Don't worry,' Sarra said brightly, 'I've asked a friend to do it. She'll be down later.' The friend was a woman with whom Sarra had worked as an air hostess years earlier. After several hours, it was clear that she wasn't coming and with heavy heart we had to climb into the van to go back to prison for the night. We would have to try to sort something out the next day.

When we returned to the prison, the other inmates started cheering as we were being taken down to our cells. I was touched that news we had been granted bail had already filtered back and these women were so happy for us. Then the prison warden on our block came to welcome us back and explained that everyone was cheering because my words with the head of human rights had worked. That afternoon, a delivery had arrived with clean sheets, blankets, pillows, God knows what. He had been as good as his word; even the warden seemed grateful.

We got back to our cell, feeling drained. Even Sarra, normally bubbly and impressively cheerful in the face of overwhelming adversity, seemed drawn. I tried to reassure her, but she broke down crying. The failure of her friend to come through with her passport as surety for our bail had finished her off.

But help was to come from another source. That night we were called up to the front office. One of the guys working on the *Tonight with Trevor McDonald* show had volunteered to offer his passport as surety, a chap called Nigel. I could have thrown my arms around him. Cynics would say it was because they wanted to do a show with Sarra and, by doing this, guaranteed themselves a world exclusive, but it's an ill wind . . .

We were taken to the World Trade Centre Hotel in Dubai, the last word in comfort. Having a shower and slipping into clean clothes, and having freshly pressed cotton sheets in bed is one of the nicest memories I have. I rang Mahmoud and told him that we had been released on bail.

I asked after the kids, and he told me that Khalid had been unwell, but that he was OK now. He said that the press had been going crazy about the story and that he'd had phone calls offering him thousands of pounds to tell his side of it. I told him not to say a word under any circumstances. If the public prosecutor saw me

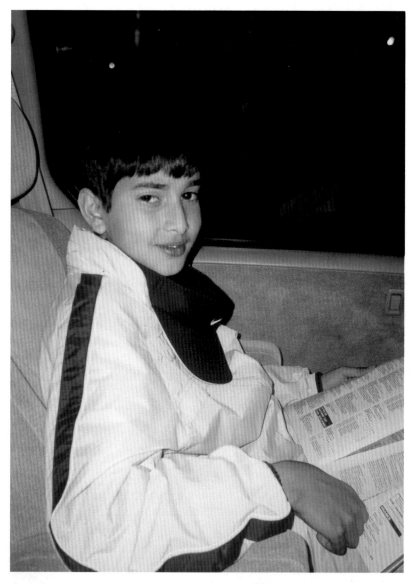

A rather tired-looking Marlon in
Whalid's car after arriving in Beirut.

Above: Khalid and Marlon amidst the luggage in the back of Alla's car on the way to rescue the children.

Below: Queuing at the border between Syria and Iraq.

Above: At last, we have crossed the border
and are heading towards Baghdad.

Below: The view from Alla's car as we travelled through Iraq.

Left: A 'petrol station'
near the border,
Iraqi-style.

Below: At the safe
house in Baghdad
after snatching the
kids.

Above: By the sea in Beirut the day after I got the kids back.

Below: The children back together having a sandwich and a coffee at the café downstairs from the Savoy Suites Hotel in Beirut.

Marlon enjoying the sun in Beirut.

Above: Khalid and Allawi playing after lunch with Whalid.

Below: At Hyde Park in London after the ordeal:
(*from left*) Khalid, Allawi, Marlon and Amira.

Amira with me and some ducks down by the Serpentine
in Hyde Park after we'd returned home.

as a professional kidnapper, I could very well be going to jail for three years.

True to his word, Mahmoud backed me up. In one interview with the *Sunday Times*, he described my role as more of a negotiator than a kidnapper, saying I was 'more like Mother Teresa than James Bond'. In the same piece, he said that he was sure that the Dubai authorities would see me for who I was, 'an angel without wings'.

So, there we were, in Dubai, free to move around, but not free to go home. The next few weeks dragged. The *Trevor McDonald* people flew Neil Fotheringham out to Dubai and staged a reunion between him and Sarra. I hated it; it was so false and staged. I had never particularly liked Neil anyway, and now I was actively growing to dislike him. I was certain that he had told the press about our plans. One paper had even printed a map of our escape route, and, as far as I knew, the only people who could have told them that were Neil and Mahmoud – and I was sure my husband wouldn't have said anything. I was getting a lot of interest from the media, who wanted to buy my story, and some of my contacts had confirmed that Neil had sold his. He had apparently told them that it had been planned, but that he had known nothing about it. I felt he was jeopardising my freedom, and, sure enough, when we went back in front of the public prosecutor, he refused to return our passports. He said that they were checking with Interpol to see if I had done this sort of thing before.

Meanwhile, Rashid's lawyers were drawing up papers to say that he would waive charges if Sarra signed custody of Tariq over to him. Despite poor Nigel's desperate entreaties to get his passport back, she refused.

Then Rashid showed a softening. He told the *Evening Standard*, 'enough with the media, enough with all this drama. If she agrees, I am willing to draft an agreement on custody of our son so she can see him whenever she wants. She cannot take the law into her own hands, and the sooner she realises the boy will live in Dubai, the sooner her problems will be over.' So, if Sarra would sign a clause agreeing not to speak to the press, she could soon be going home.

That didn't mean I would be, though. They could still decide to make an example of me. I decided to appeal to the highest authority in the land, Sheikh Al Maktoum, the ruler of Dubai and Abu Dhabi. We drafted a letter, saying that we were very sorry for what we had done and that we would never do it again, if I could just be allowed to go home to my husband and sick child.

The next day, we were sitting in the hotel reception area having a coffee with a lady from the law firm who was representing us when there was something of a commotion. In swept some bodyguards, followed by a small group of men. It was Sheikh Al Maktoum himself. They stayed in a knot around him and escorted him into a private dining room, before taking up position outside the door. I went up to them and begged to be allowed to give him my letter, but they refused, saying that we would have to petition his court, a process that could take a very long time. I beseeched them, but they were immovable.

At last, realising nothing we could say would change their minds, we sat down again and kept an eye on the door. After a couple of hours, it opened and the Sheikh came out. We jumped up and tried to approach with the letter, but the bodyguards stepped in front of us. The Sheikh, however, waved them away, asking what we wanted. We told him that we had a letter for him.

He indicated a man next to him, saying, 'Mr Kalifah will take care of this.'

The man gave us a mobile-phone number and told us to call him in a few minutes. We rang ten minutes later and he told us that the sheikh supported our petition. We could pick up our passports from the attorney general's office the next morning.

We had done it! Unbelievably, we had bypassed the court process and effectively been pardoned by the highest authority in the land.

The next day, we collected our passports. We were free to go home.

Chapter 8

Stepping Into the Spotlight

I had been in Dubai with Sarra Fotheringham for seven weeks. When I came back, the media went mad. I was being recognised in the street, which was weird, since I had done all my work in secrecy before that. These women needed help, not publicity – having your face splashed across the front pages of newspapers doesn't always help, as I had learned in Dubai.

A lady came up to me as we came through arrivals and gave me a hug, saying, 'Welcome back. Keep up the good work.' She must have seen my picture in the papers. I also received flowers from two female reporters. I had sold an exclusive story to a Sunday newspaper when I was out in Dubai, so one of their journalists was waiting at the airport. He met us off the plane, led us to a car and took us home. When I got there, I spent the night with the children, which was absolute heaven. I was so grateful to be back, and, of the course, the children were delighted, clambering all over me and whooping with excitement.

The following day I met up with the journalist again. I had first met him in Dubai when he'd been out doing an article on Sarra. He paid them £20,000 to do the story, and he paid it upfront. But then he met me, and wanted my story too. Everything seemed fine and we sorted the whole thing out. He didn't want me to talk to anyone until the Sunday, when they'd run their story – I think this was on a Wednesday.

Some of the papers had run stories which presented me as the one who was innocent, and as a result people were ringing up the embassy in Dubai saying, 'Let Donya go, she's done nothing.' I heard later that the Foreign Office was also being inundated with calls. But at the end of the day, we had planned to use false passports – I was going to use my son's passport for Tariq. We all knew we were doing something wrong. The story that was published the day we got arrested showed details of our plans. They knew we were heading for Basra, they knew everything. Indeed, I believe it was this story which upset the authorities. I'll never know for certain, but that's what I believe.

That weekend, though, just after we arrived home, someone else ran the story – the *Daily Mirror*, I think – so the journalist I'd spoken to thought I'd done a deal behind his paper's back and was very upset with me. Then again, I wasn't too happy with him – he had run Neil's story in the first place and had caused a lot of trouble for me. I believe that was one big factor in us being put in prison, so I was mad.

I found out from another journalist that Neil was trying to sell stories to anyone who would pay. He was just thinking about the money; he didn't appreciate the seriousness of the situation. He didn't think Sarra would be arrested for taking her own child.

I was now learning to swim with sharks. They say, bring a long spoon if you want to sup with the Devil, and that's what it felt like with these reporters. Many journalists are very nice people, but a lot of them are under incredible pressure to get a story and will resort to anything to do it. For example, there was another newspaper that ran a piece without my permission, although I had spoken to the journalist involved. We never saw a penny for it. When I was in Dubai, she had faxed me an offer, saying if we spoke to them, they would give us £8,000, so I signed it and faxed it back. But, of course, she ran the story and then said that she never received the fax. That's what you have to deal with from the newspapers and it's made me a lot harder, a lot less trusting.

Not all are bad, though, and I became friendly with some of them, in particular Sharon Hendry, the women's editor at *The Sun*. She invited me to the Woman of the Year awards. I took Amira, and she was wide-eyed at everything. I was sitting with Noel Edmonds and there were Page 3 girls everywhere. It was at The Roof Gardens in Kensington, a very swanky venue in west London, with ponds with flamingos and all sorts up there on top of a tall block of offices. It was fantastic. I also took Bill Shepperton from Shepperton Studios, who was interested in making a film about my experiences. Suddenly, I was meeting all these glamorous people – I even chatted to Melinda Messenger, who was pregnant at the time – and maybe it was going to my head a little. But the awards were about rewarding ordinary people, and it was great to see everyday people being recognised. It made me realise how lucky I was to have my kids, and that's what I was thinking that day.

I got in the lift to go back down to the car with Bill, and Cherie Blair, the Prime Minister's wife, was in the lift with her bodyguard. She was chatting away to my daughter, saying what a lovely handbag she had. Noel Edmonds also got in the lift. During the event, he'd been talking about losing his mother and saying he felt very strongly about a mother's bond with her children.

In the lift, he told me he'd seen me in the papers, so I made a joke about it to Cherie, saying, 'I've just been in the same place as your husband – Iraq.' Tony Blair had just been out to see the soldiers at that time. 'We all came back in one piece, so let's hope everyone else does,' I added. Then Cherie realised who I was and said, 'Keep up the good work.' She was a very classy lady and seemed the sort to say exactly what she meant. And, of course, she loved Amira, so I loved her for that.

* * *

When I first got back, I was so happy to see Mahmoud and the kids; he had kept the family going. He was my rock. We'd had our ups and downs like every normal couple, but now things really started to go wrong. I think once you go to prison – even for a short period of time – your life changes. You realise that there are so many difficulties with your life, and you find out who you really are when you're on your own, when you're not with your children. I had got married, had my kids . . . never really had any time for myself. Not as an adult, anyway. I'd spent the last few years trying to be a good wife and a good mother, not really thinking about *my* needs. I think that's when things really started to go wrong.

Then I had seven weeks in Dubai, ironically having a bit of freedom. Although, in theory, I was under arrest, I was free in the sense that I didn't have the kids around – I could focus on myself and think about what was going on without any other distractions – although I was pining for them. It's a bit like when you take puppies away from the mother, she goes mad, and I think maybe I had been a little bit like that.

Even though they had my passport in Dubai, I could move around. Emotionally and mentally, I had not been free because every day I was scared; I constantly felt sick, as though the situation was going to engulf me. I would wake up every morning with butterflies in my stomach, and it was the same at the end of the day when I went to bed. I'd be sitting in a restaurant thinking, 'I just want to go home.'

Whenever you are somewhere you don't want to be, you want to be carrying your passport and free. When you're in these countries on these jobs, your passport represents freedom and control, an opportunity to get back to your real life. Having it taken away, you feel you've lost all control. That's your life, that passport – without it you're in trouble. Many journalists have been arrested in some of these countries because they've been accused of spying; you have to know the rules and regulations. In Dubai, for example, if you drink alcohol outside your hotel (not that I drink), you could be arrested. People don't explain these rules to you when you visit these countries, you're supposed to know what they are. You don't expect Dubai to be like that, you think it's such a friendly nation, accepting of Western values, very popular now with British tourists. But underneath it's still the same as any other Middle Eastern country. You have to know what's what.

I learned that about Dubai from seeing those other women in the prison, and hearing the things they were in for. Some were relatively serious offences, of course, but others were things that would just get you a caution in the UK. While I was out in Dubai, I began to re-evaluate things back home. I decided not to take things for granted so much, not to allow myself to get so stressed, so manic. I resolved to spend more time with the children, to sit down with them more often, and to talk to them and listen more attentively. I wanted to analyse things more rather than just rush into them. I'd said yes to the whole Fotheringham thing without thinking it through. I had believed Sarra and taken her at face value. After spending time with her, I realised I had made a serious error in judgement.

In Dubai, with all that time on my hands, I also started thinking about my relationship with Mahmoud. I was thinking that my marriage wasn't everything I wanted it to be. Maybe I was too dependent on him, maybe I was thinking too much about the kids and not enough about my needs. The fact was I had rushed into marriage both times. Our relationship had become a habit, an everyday routine based around the children, and less of a connection between him and me. There had once been a time when Mahmoud and I would not be parted from one another. Then it all seemed to just fall apart. Mahmoud was never what I would call a romantic person – although, of course, he would do nice things. However, taking Allawi and Amira away from me, as he would do later, obliterated everything that had come before.

My next trip took me to Iran and while I was there he wrote to me telling me to look after myself, and how much he loved me. I've kept all those letters. And yet while I was away, he was planning his move, planning to abduct our children, getting passports for the kids. So it was all premeditated. This is what makes me mad about these men. Things that are premeditated must be organised coldly, out of spite. They're not done out of a misguided sense of goodwill, or of what might be best for the children. To me, if you do something that is premeditated, it is wrong. If you carry out a crime on the spur of the moment or have a huge row with someone, that's one thing. But to plan it, and carry it out in cold blood, that's wrong.

But, of course, at this stage I had no idea what he was going to do. In Dubai, I still believed he was a good dad, that he would do anything for the children, and I thought he still loved me because my absence seemed to be making him suffer. He had to put up with a lot while I was in Dubai and I think that broke up our marriage because he couldn't take it any more. The media didn't really help matters because they were ringing him up, offering him money for his story. He was offered up to £25,000, which is a hell of a lot of money to anyone, especially someone who works as a waiter, but I told him not to talk to anybody, and, of course, he didn't – except to say good things that would help my case.

The media attention was taking over my life. I was getting all kinds of offers from the press and invitations to go on *GMTV*, *Richard and Judy* and *Trisha* in the UK, and *60 Minutes* in America. But I'd had enough and just wanted to spend time with the children, so we took them on holiday that December. In the run-up to this trip, I spent lots of time with the children. The community was great; they rallied round. My neighbour was asked to go on *Kilroy* to talk about me, but she said no. They were very supportive.

The previous year, I had decided I needed to put all my thoughts down on paper. I got in touch with a ghost writer named Andrew Crofts and asked him to write my book with me, and from then on started keeping a note of everything. I remember the first day he came to my house was 11 September 2001, the day of the awful Twin Towers atrocity. I was upstairs recording with him when Mahmoud shouted, 'Come down and see this.' Andrew was so upset he called his wife. We didn't know what was going on; we thought maybe Britain would be attacked. Andrew wanted to leave to go home and be with his family, which was understandable. He lives down in Sussex. I went and got my kids out of school.

Now, over a year later, Andrew had almost finished the book, so I was talking with him on the phone a lot and doing interviews. Added to this, there was all the attention from other media, which meant whatever little free time I had was spent with the children. In hindsight, I should have realised that my relationship with Mahmoud was souring. We were rowing the whole time, and I think he was growing resentful of all the attention I was getting. Like many Middle Eastern men, he is proud, and working as a waiter in a restaurant while I was being phoned by television companies and newspapers probably made him feel insecure. But, of course, I didn't read the danger signs. During one argument, I had even hinted that it may be time to think about divorce, which probably hit him hard.

At this time, a television production company called Shine, which is owned by Rupert Murdoch's daughter Elisabeth, got in touch. They are very successful at making TV documentaries and wanted to do one on child abduction. I arranged a meeting with one of the producers, an American lady named Monica Garnsey. She came to my house and explained what they intended to do. They had contacted a lady named Alison Lalic, who was in her mid-30s and lived in Liverpool. She had met a Bosnian man named Ramiz on holiday in Yugoslavia and had married him. Seven years previously, he had abducted their two little girls and taken them back to Bosnia. Shine wanted to take a film crew out there to see if they could track down the children – and they wanted me to go with them.

I agreed to meet Alison the next day at Café Rouge in Whiteleys.

I was absolutely devastated when I heard her story; I felt so sorry for her. She had gone on holiday to Yugoslavia in 1989, when she was just 23. She had met a handsome local lad at a disco and they had had a holiday fling. After returning home, they maintained the relationship by phone, and she had gone back out there in January 1990 to marry Ramiz. They went to live in the small village on the north-west border of Bosnia where he was from and where his brothers and sisters lived. The family had welcomed Alison, but living in such a tiny village in the middle of nowhere had been a culture shock, and work opportunities were few and far between.

After six months, they moved back to the UK and settled in Liverpool, Alison's home town. They bought a house and very quickly had a little girl they called Samantha. Two years later, they had Rebecca.

'He was a very good father,' Alison said, 'and he absolutely doted on his little girls.'

But in 1992, war broke out in Bosnia. Ramiz was a Muslim, and his brothers fought on the front line. Suddenly, there was a great change in him. He had never been particularly religious, but after the war he became a devout Muslim and went to mosque every day. Alison felt that he was becoming a stranger, that he was not the man she had married.

It was a story I was all too familiar with, and it fitted in perfectly with my observations of Muslim men and how they turn their backs on the loose morals of the West, particularly when they have little girls. Had I known Alison at the time, I could have seen that this was a textbook situation and that her children were in grave danger. But, of course, I didn't.

As well as closing himself off from Alison, Ramiz became cold and unpleasant to her, and their marriage became joyless and loveless. Things limped along until 1995, when Alison divorced Ramiz. She was awarded custody of the children and, for a few months, things seemed fine. Despite the separation, Ramiz continued to be a thoughtful and responsible father, with frequent visits and contact.

That summer, he asked for Alison's permission to take the girls on holiday to Germany, where his parents were living. He wanted them to see their grandchildren, and Alison, a kind person, didn't refuse what seemed to be a reasonable request. But, of course, they never returned.

You may think it was naive, but a lot of people don't expect anything like this to happen, as it's not publicised enough. People make documentaries on the TV, for example, but not enough people watch them; this sort of thing just doesn't get enough publicity. There's an organisation in the UK called REUNITE which aims to help in cases of child abduction, but as I've stressed so many times, they can only give advice about what to do. They are part-funded by the Department for Constitutional Affairs, the Foreign and Commonwealth Office and the Home Office, and will only act strictly within the letter of the law. They can't go in and help you get your children back – no one can – they can only tell you the legal or practical side. If the father refuses to give them back, there's very little anyone can do.

Alison grew frantic and took to phoning Ramiz's brother Safit's house every day. It transpired that he had taken them back to Bosnia, and she knew they were there. For months, he refused to speak to her, or to allow her to speak to the children no matter how much she pleaded and begged. They were no longer Samantha and Rebecca, he told her, inflicting another cruel blow; they were now known by their Muslim names: Aisha and Safija.

After four months of this, he relented and said that she could speak to them, but then always contrived to find an excuse. They would be at a friend's house doing homework, or they were in bed, or they had forgotten how to speak English. The poor woman was distraught.

She took her case to court, and an international warrant went out for Ramiz's arrest. As I explained earlier, if a country is a signatory of the Hague Convention, child abduction is a criminal offence domestically, so the Bosnian authorities should have been trying to track him down. Given that his brother was a policeman, it shouldn't have been too difficult, but clearly the family had done everything they could to protect him from the authorities, and nothing had happened.

By now, her daughters would have been about ten and twelve. She'd been over to Bosnia some years earlier with a BBC crew after someone said they had seen them. She went to the house where they thought the kids were, but there was no sign of them. Despite the fact that she had been awarded full custody of the children by the courts through an international warrant, there was nothing the Government could do. Ramiz was wanted on charges of child abduction, so he was hardly going to just turn up and say, 'Oh, sorry, there you go.'

Of course Alison was beside herself telling me this story, and I found it upsetting too. After the problems I'd had in Dubai six months previously, I had resolved not to get involved. Before I met Alison, I had told Monica I only wanted to act as a consultant for the documentary, that I didn't want to go out to Bosnia myself, but after seeing Alison, I found it impossible to say no. I took a deep breath, tried not to think about what Mahmoud was going to say and said, 'OK, if they're in Bosnia, we'll find them.'

Of course, everyone from Shine was delighted, as was Alison. But when I told Mahmoud, he didn't really react. He just shook his head, and said, 'I suppose I'll be looking after the children again. What do you want me to tell them this time?' He wasn't happy, I could see that, but at least he didn't fly off the handle.

I met up again with the Shine people. As well as Monica, there was another producer called Paul Hamann, whom I really liked. He was a tall chap with a posh accent, and was very good at putting people at ease. And there was another woman called Michelle Ross, who worked as an assistant producer. We all got on very well, and I came to regard them as friends.

We decided to see what we could find out before we flew a whole film crew out, so we signed Edin, a Bosnian guy whom we found through contacts with a Sunday newspaper, as a fixer – he was supposed to do some sniffing around and find out if the kids were there before we went to all the expense of flying everyone out. After a few days, we heard back from him. He told us he'd seen the kids and that they were at a school near Bihac, a town in the north-west corner of the country. We were game on.

This time it wasn't too much of a wrench to say goodbye to the kids. The mission was strictly above board, completely legal – we had international law on our side. Best of all, we had agreed that we would only be going for three days. It should have been reasonably straightforward.

We all flew to Sarajevo – me, Monica, Michelle, Alison, Alison's brother Darren and a friend of mine, Maria, who's married to an Iraqi guy. There were also a few cameramen, so we kind of stood out. We arrived on 30 November 2002.

When we arrived in Bosnia, the Customs officials checked all our equipment. They seemed slightly suspicious, but Monica explained that we were a British documentary crew doing a film about Bosnia and its reconstruction after the war. They seemed happy with our explanation and they let us through.

Outside, we met up with the fixers, including Edin – or 'Head On' as we came to call him, as he seemed to rush headlong into everything. He reminded me of the guy in *Jurassic Park* with the goatee beard who stuffs his face all the time. They had arranged a van for us, a Volkswagen with sliding doors, the sort you see Australian backpackers using to travel around Europe. I was going to start singing the theme tune to *Scooby Doo*, but I thought I'd better not. Bright orange! I made some quip about how we might as well go the whole hog and write 'UN' on the side, but it wasn't funny really – the last thing you want to be doing on an undercover operation is standing out like a sore thumb, but it was too late to do anything about it.

I have to be honest and say that I hated Bosnia. It was really depressing. It was freezing and really grey. The only thing I remember that was good was the countryside – it would have been beautiful had it not been in the deep of winter. I remember lakes and rivers that were almost green, or aquamarine. We drove along winding roads by lakes, through tunnels that had been carved into the mountains, through passes . . . I'm sure if I went back in the summer, I would find it incredibly beautiful. But with the snow and the freezing air, it was hard to enjoy the scenery. And whenever we came to a village or town, there were bullet- and bomb-damaged buildings everywhere to remind you of the country's terrible recent history. There was nothing in one piece.

We got to Bihac, where we were staying, shortly after it got dark. We found the hotel, but it was a bit of a dump. It looked like a '60s polytechnic from the outside and, inside, it reminded me of something out of *The Shining*. It was all long marble corridors. We checked in and had a quick conference. I said I'd like to see the school that night from where we going to snatch the kids so that we'd be set up the next day and know exactly what to expect. Monica and Michelle agreed, but Edin wasn't too happy. Still, Shine was paying him, so he was overruled.

Edin drove us to the building where we were told the children were staying, about 10 minutes away. From their house, there was a long hill down to the village and secondary school. This hill was reasonably busy with traffic and there was little in the way of safety for children who might be walking there. There was not even a proper pavement – it was unbelievable to think that kids would be walking down it at 7 a.m. or 8 a.m. in the dark to get to school. It wasn't like London, where you daren't take your eyes off your children – kids seemed so independent there. This was out in the countryside. It was the nearby primary school which we would be watching, though.

Edin said we should park outside the school and snatch the kids on their way in. 'You must be joking,' I said. 'There's going to be loads of kids, it's snowing, we are very unlikely to recognise them and, even if we do, we need to get out of there fast, which we can't do in these driving conditions. It's not just a case of putting them in the van, we need to watch for a few days to work out which ones are the right kids.'

So, we decided to move cautiously – to get a clear idea of where everything was and the route the children would be taking to get to school – then went back to the hotel. We went to bed and got up at 5 a.m. to go back and stake out the school. I went into Alison's room to check whether she was ready for what we were going to be doing, and she seemed up for it. I was a bit worried about Darren, though. He was going to be driving the van and would effectively be the getaway driver. When I asked him if he was ready for what needed to be done, he didn't seem at all happy about it. I think he was probably concerned that we were in their territory and that Safit was a policeman. It didn't help that Alison had told us that when she was living here, everyone seemed to have guns and didn't seem scared to use them. It's all very well knowing a country's signed up to the Hague Convention, but when you're in the middle of nowhere that doesn't give you great peace of mind.

At last, though, he said he would do whatever was necessary. We needed to get there early, as kids started arriving from about 7.30, so we took no risks and got there at 6.45 a.m. We had pulled the curtains in the van and peeped out every so often. Monica and Michelle were in another car and we had walkie-talkies to stay in touch. We saw some kids walking past us, going down to the main school, but there was no one going into the primary school. We were watching and watching, but there was no sign of any kids. I got on the walkie-talkie and said, 'There's no one going into the primary school, are you sure it's not a holiday?' At 8.30 or so, we had to abandon the mission as it wasn't going anywhere, and we were worried about drawing attention to ourselves.

It turned out later that the primary school at the top of the hill had been closed down for a year, only the main school was open and the younger children had been absorbed into that school. How the hell had Edin seen these kids, then? It didn't add up.

We headed back to Bihac and went to the hotel for some breakfast and a conference. Alison was distraught; the morning had been a setback for her. She kept crying, saying things like, 'How can he be so cruel? Those girls are my flesh and blood. They'll think that I don't care, that I have no heart.'

I sat and talked to her for a while, telling her not to give up. I told her about some of my previous mums who had got their children back, in the hope that it would give her some encouragement, but she was very down that morning.

The trouble with the village we were staking out was that it had been home to Ramiz's family for generations, and the inhabitants of these places have incredible loyalty to one another. Since Ramiz had come home with the girls, he'd married a local girl and naturally the village had closed ranks around them. As far as they were concerned, Alison was just a troublemaker from a far-off country. I suppose if the same thing had happened in a tiny village in the north of England or somewhere, and a Bosnian girl kept turning up demanding her children, people would be reluctant to get involved. That said, because of the police and court system in the UK, that situation wouldn't arise. We seem to play by the rules far more than many other countries.

Alison had actually been out to the village on three previous occasions trying to track down her girls, but to no avail. The closest she ever came was seeing a photograph of them, which made her convinced that the trail started here. One of the saddest things was when she said that coming back to this cruel, hostile village somehow made her feel closer to her children.

She had had one or two people trying to help, though. 'It's such a tight-knit community,' she said. 'People say they have seen the girls, but as soon as the police are involved, they're scared.'

That afternoon, we went to the brother's house. He lived in one of three buildings next to each other in a field. I got out and walked about arm-in-arm with Michelle. Safit's home was nothing out of the ordinary: a two-storey house with a graveyard behind and an alley to get to the graveyard. I was talking into my mike and had these special glasses on with hidden cameras.

'Look, these kids aren't here, there's no sign of them,' I whispered. You get a sixth sense for these things. There were no toys about, no little dolls' prams. But no one would believe me.

The next morning, we had another pointless trip to wait around outside the school, but, of course, there was no sign of the girls. I was getting frustrated now, and I was angry with Edin because I felt he had led us on a merry goose chase. I said I wasn't going to hang around aimlessly when there was no sign of any kids, and told Edin to back off as he'd cocked up.

Edin said he'd seen these kids in the house and at the school but he couldn't have done; as far as I could see, he'd just lied to get his money. However, Safit still lived in that house and his kids attended the school. I thought that, if anything happened at the school, the kids would come home and tell their parents, so we decided to go into the school and raise the stakes.

We went in and spoke to the headmaster. They brought Safit's daughter in to see us. Edin had arranged for an interpreter to be there, but I thought she was very rude, very blunt and abrupt in her questioning, and I didn't like her at all. She wasn't asking the questions in the way we wanted them asked, she wasn't simply translating. You have to know how to talk to children, but she was so aggressive that the little girl was frightened. Alison was crying, asking if she'd seen her daughters, but the girl was saying that she hadn't seen them for ages. The headmaster said that no one knew where they were, but Alison was just convinced that everyone was lying to cover up for Ramiz.

Then the school caretaker came forward and said he wanted to speak to us. He was a lovely old guy, very kind. He said, through the interpreter, 'I understand what she's doing,' gesturing towards Alison. 'I would do the same for my kids.' He explained that Aisha and Safija had been at the school, but only for a few months. Ramiz had taken them out, but he didn't know where they'd gone. He promised that the moment he heard anything, he would get in touch. He finished by saying, 'Tell her not to cry. They're not sad, they're good kids.'

It was clear then that the headmaster had known more than he had let on, and that Alison was right to fear a conspiracy, a wall of silence. It was very sad watching Alison going around the school, sitting on chairs and saying that maybe it was the same one on which one of the girls had sat. It was like watching someone drowning.

I had decided on our next plan of action. 'What we need to do now is go into the house and install a listening device because when that little girl gets home, the first thing she's going to do is tell her parents everything and we need to know what they're saying.'

Edin, of course, got really scared and responded with, 'No, we can't do it, it's illegal, we could go to prison.' So he was no use.

But one of the cameramen, a guy called Richard, was in support. 'OK, I'll go in with you and help you do it, if it comes to it.'

I wanted Edin to do it really; he was being paid to be a fixer and all he'd fixed for us so far was to drive around in some stupid *Scooby Doo* van. This argument was going on in the car. Eventually, Edin, Alison and I went up to the house with the listening device all set up and knocked on the door. This was where Safit lived.

They invited us in and were quite friendly. They offered us a drink, but I said I was fasting, as it was Ramadan at the time. I just wanted to get the listening device installed. I was looking around to see if there was any evidence of the girls in the house, any photos of them standing in front of a landmark; not that I was looking for pictures of Brighton Pier or anything, just something that might help. There was nothing like that, but there were framed verses from the Koran. These sorts of things are from the Middle East, so there was a clue.

While they were talking to us, we slipped the device under the table. Alison was crying, begging them for any information, but they were reluctant to tell us anything.

He eventually admitted that Ramiz sometimes phoned, but that he had no number for him; they could only wait for him to ring. They came out with some rubbish about how he never called from the same number and that he only rang every three months or so and, no, they didn't know which country he was in. They finished by saying that if they heard anything, they would let us know. So we left.

Then we started listening to what they said afterwards, and they were scared. They didn't trust me at all, nor Edin, and they didn't buy our story that we were concerned friends. They thought we were undercover. Undercover what, I don't know, and they didn't say. Then we could hear the little girl coming in from school. You could hear her say, 'Hi, Mum, hi, Dad, guess what? Today this lady came into the school with Alison . . .' She told the whole story. You could hear it all. But the problem was we had to go back to change the cassette every 45 minutes. We'd stashed the tape recorder in the graveyard at the back of the building so that it would be within range. It was like something out of *The Blair Witch Project* – we were stumbling around in the dark with these spyglasses on that made your eyes look really white. Only Richard and Michelle had the balls to come and change the tapes. Edin, of course, wouldn't do it.

Anyway, lo and behold, they rang Ramiz and told him Alison had been there looking for the children. Alison had previously sold their old house in Liverpool and Safit was telling him to use her desperation to get some of the money from her, and to convince her to sign a legal agreement giving up custody of the children and handing it to him. He suggested that, in return, she could see the kids. That is how cruel people can be, trading on the misery of others and exploiting it for financial gain.

Over the next couple of days, there were more calls from Ramiz. We kept sneaking back to change the tapes, and would bring them back to the hotel for Edin to translate. Once, after Michelle and

Richard arrived back with the latest instalment, Edin came running out of his room, shouting, 'We have to leave tonight! They found the listening device!'

One of the children had found the bug. You could hear the mother saying, 'What's this?' and then the tape went dead.

They called me out of bed at this point for a conference. I looked like Rip Van Winkle in a long nightrobe with a woolly hat, scarf and boots – it was freezing in that hotel. Edin wanted us to leave that night, but I put my foot down. 'No way,' I said. 'We'll leave in the morning. She's a village woman, she's not going to know it's a listening device, she'll probably think it's something off the video.' We went back to bed and in the morning all agreed there was no point in hanging around. It was obvious the kids weren't there.

Before we headed back to London, we decided to spend a couple of days visiting an orphanage in Mostar, a town in the south-west, reasonably close to Sarajevo. We took food and presents, and it was one of the most wonderful experiences of my life. It was a beautiful orphanage. Suzanne Mubarak, the wife of the Egyptian President, had built it and attended the opening ceremony. Each little house or chalet that the children were living in had the name of the pyramids or something else to do with Egypt. There was a gym there as well, which was great. There was a shortage of food – there always is – but the living conditions were wonderful. I took a shine to one little girl of about 13 who wouldn't let go of her teddy. They thought I was a princess from England, like Lady Di, because I brought a load of sweets and chocolates. Each chalet had a sitting room with a dormitory upstairs. It had been built near a breathtaking waterfall which was so high up, and the chalets overlooked this. We spent about three hours there, playing with the children, then walked across the Mostar Bridge. The next day, 6 December, we flew home.

Alison was very upset, almost heartbroken. She was a quiet, petite woman, about 36 years old, who worked as a nursery nurse. She had been very depressed and coming home without the kids had been a severe blow to her. She had set a great deal of store by our trip and had hoped for a better result. When we got back, we got phone records through for Safit's house. We could see that when they had phoned Ramiz, the number was the same one. They phoned it every Friday.

It was a residential number in Tehran, in Iran. That was a much more serious mission, and one that I did not know whether I could face. It is strictly sharia law in that country, and I shuddered to think what they might do to a British woman who was trying to snatch two little girls from their father.

Mahmoud's immediate reaction was quite forceful. 'You're bloody well not going to Iran! They'll execute you out there if you get caught.'

I said I was going anyway, so he said, 'Suit yourself.' Looking back, maybe this was when he started to hatch his plan.

We had Christmas together and I decided to go in the New Year. Michelle was out there already doing some preliminary work, organising visas and so on. She managed to track down the area of Tehran where they were staying and even managed to film them outside a block of flats playing on roller skates. She emailed this recording back and Monica arranged for Alison to come to my flat to watch the footage on a laptop. It was so sad. She knew it was her daughters straight away. She was convinced they looked unhappy in the photo, but I think she might have been reading more into it than was there. She probably had a powerful need to believe they were unhappy, rather than to accept that they might have forgotten about her and were getting on with their own lives.

After all these years of searching, though, she finally knew where her children were. She crumpled up and started sobbing, but more through relief than despair. I started crying too, and said, 'Don't worry, we'll go out there and get them.'

Then, three days later, on 29 January 2003, we were on a plane to Tehran via Munich. We had spoken to a contact at the Foreign Office, but off the record they told us that if they made any enquiries, it would simply alert Ramiz to the fact that Alison, or the authorities, had managed to track him down. Instead, we just travelled like tourists.

On the plane, I was sitting next to a tall chap with an American accent. We got chatting, and he said he was a freelance journalist. My life seemed to be full of journalists these days, and it was causing problems between me and Mahmoud. I didn't know it yet, but so would this one. But he was lovely, and charming. We swapped numbers, and he said he would get in touch when he was back in London, where he was usually based.

Tehran was a culture shock. I had always imagined Iran to be a romantic country – I had visions of ancient Persia and all that – but it was completely snowbound and freezing. We were struggling to get the cars along the road. We checked into our hotel, and the next day we headed to the flats where the children had been seen. I had to hang around outside the building for two hours each morning to watch for these kids in case they went to school. The flat was situated in a pleasant enough suburb of Tehran, with decent flats and nice shops, but I was so cold – if you'd put a stick up my backside, I'd have been an ice lolly. I had been sitting in the car for what felt like an age with Monica, Michelle, Alison and the driver we'd hired. Eventually, I had to get out, just to feel like I was doing something. I started walking around the area, trying to find things out. Once, I went into a shop to get a packet of biscuits and told the shopkeeper I was moving to Tehran and that my husband was going to be lecturing at the university.

One of the advantages of wearing the hijab is that everyone is really friendly. They know you're a Muslim, so they warm to you. I thought the Iranian people were lovely, really friendly, and felt bad that we were not who we said we were, that we were sneaking around in an underhand way, but sometimes you have to do these things for the greater good.

We had found out that Ramiz was living in one of these flats with a Bosnian wife and two little girls. Despite the fact that he had about as many qualifications as me – that is, none – he had managed to get a job at Tehran University, and the neighbours called him the 'Bosnian Professor'. One morning we followed him, which is no easy feat in Tehran, with deep snow and traffic and everything else. We managed it, though, and were able to ascertain that to get to work he took two buses, which took him about an hour. It was good news for us – we didn't want him nearby and able to get back at a moment's notice. It was Alison who had first spotted him that morning, leaving for work early with his briefcase. She stiffened and said, 'That's him, that's Ramiz!' She was obviously scared of him.

We were watching a particular flat and we hadn't seen anything for two days, so on the third day I told Monica that I thought we were watching the wrong flat. She and I had a row about it, and I got out of the car, saying, 'Right, I'm going to see if they're in that flat.'

She was convinced we had the right one, but I knew we would have seen them if they'd been there. I love Monica, it was just that things were a bit tense because of the pressure of what we were doing, the fear of getting caught, plus we were really tired. We were all doing our best.

Michelle and I started having a snowball fight and joined in playing with kids in the street. Because of the severe weather, and the thick snow on the roads, most kids seemed to have an unofficial holiday. I got chatting to one little boy and asked him where he was from. He said he was from India and that his father was working in Tehran. I said to him that there had been two little girls playing with my daughter a few days before – did he know where they were? He told me that they lived in a different block – we *were* watching the wrong block.

He pointed up to a flat on the third floor, so we took the car round and carried on playing in the street, making lots of noise. Out of the corner of my eye, I was keeping an eye on the flat and saw the curtain move. There was a little girl, a miniature version of

Alison. I smiled at her and she smiled back, but in a slightly cagey way. We carried on playing and eventually they came down and joined in, throwing snowballs. I was playing around with them, rolling around in the snow. They thought we were mad. They didn't speak any English.

Then suddenly we saw Alison walking towards us. She went right up to the kids, but they didn't know who she was, so she leaned down beside them and started trying to show them a bracelet that one of them had owned, that she hoped they would recognise. She had put great hope into them recognising the bracelet, even if they didn't immediately recognise her. But there was no spark there. Samantha, or Aisha, the older of the two girls, started throwing snowballs really violently at her, so I said to Monica that we should get out of there immediately. By now, a man had come out to see what was going on and I began to get scared. I certainly didn't want to get picked up by Tehran police. So we all got into the car and went back to the hotel in the city centre.

We sat down to discuss what to do. The problem was that it was clear that these girls didn't recognise Alison, so we couldn't just snatch them. Imagine what would happen if two little girls were snatched by strangers in this country? They'd be screaming, the police would be called, God knows what. So it was a big concern. Alison, of course, was distraught. She had finally seen her kids and they didn't recognise her, didn't want her.

There was nothing more that I could do, so I flew home the next day. Monica and Michelle stayed out there with Alison. I saw the rushes – the unedited footage they had taken – when they came home, and it was heartbreaking. Alison kept ringing the flat, and when one of the little girls answered, she would try to speak to them in her few words of Arabic. But the little girls kept saying things like, 'Don't call us, stop bothering us.'

She got through to Ramiz and begged him not to hang up, that she would give him half the money from the house and sign over custody to him if he would move back to Bosnia and let her see the children. There was a pause, and then he hung up.

Shine somehow contacted Ramiz to ask his permission for Alison to see the girls. By now, he had moved some 12 hours away. He agreed, but only on the condition that Alison went by herself. He kept his word and took Alison to see the girls. They met and travelled by coach to his home. We received a letter from her saying it was great; that it was the first time in almost eight years that she had felt like a mum.

When she came home a week or two later, I met her and she was happy. She had made contact. She had also instructed the authorites to drop the charges against Ramiz. Later, I heard that she had gone back out there and that the girls were calling her Mum. He apparently agreed that, when they are older, if they want to come back to the UK for college or whatever, they can do so. You have to bear in mind that they had been apart for a long time, so these things have to happen gradually. That's a risk she's prepared to take. I mean, they're calling her Mum now, which is a big step forward. She's getting her life back and her kids want to be with her. All children want to be with their mum. If you're taken away when you're two or four, it's very hard to remember so it takes work to rebuild that bond. I can't remember what happened to me when I was four and I doubt anyone else can. But the need is there, the desire is there in those little girls, and it can be built on.

Life is sometimes cruel, but that's the way it is.

Chapter 9

My World Caves In

When I came back from Tehran, it was back to normal life. Mahmoud and I were like strangers living under the same roof. We hardly spoke, except to bicker, and I couldn't see where we could go from there. William, the chap I'd met on the plane, got in touch and asked me out to lunch, and I thought, 'Why not?' We had a nice time and met up every few days for coffee, or a walk. It was good to have some companionship, but nothing was happening. He was a good friend – nothing more.

Naturally, though, Mahmoud didn't see it that way. He muttered stuff under his breath and was quite hostile if William ever came round to the flat. The kids, though, adored him, and Mahmoud knew nothing was going on really. For one thing, I wouldn't have had time. Between dropping the kids off, doing the shopping and collecting them from school, there weren't enough hours in the day. It was just another stick for Mahmoud to beat over my head. During the few weeks that followed, Mahmoud and I were as distant as we had ever been.

I was on a high from all the things going on in my life: Shine were putting the documentary together and Andrew Crofts had finished writing my first book, which would be coming out soon. I felt that I was developing and that my life was beginning to take off, and I think that Mahmoud felt threatened by this. I chose to ignore it, though, as there was little that I could do about it.

And then came Tuesday, 25 March, the day that changed my life. Mahmoud was taking the two youngest children to the dentist in the morning. He'd phoned me up and said, 'Allawi is not being good and won't go to school, so I'm going to take him to the dentist with us when I take Amira.' She was going to the Eastman Dental Hospital on Gray's Inn Road in King's Cross because she'd had a problem with a couple of her back teeth and they needed to come out. Mahmoud was supposedly taking her to have them treated.

That day, I was meeting up with someone from the Scottish edition of *The Sun*. It was a female reporter who wanted to do a feature on cases of mothers having their children abducted and she wanted to interview me. I arranged to meet her at – you guessed it – Café Rouge in Whiteleys. We were there for around three hours, had some lunch, then carried on doing the interview. Throughout the afternoon I'd tried to ring Mahmoud's mobile, but it was switched off. I wanted to check on Amira, but I wasn't unduly concerned; I had no reason to suspect anything. In the afternoon, I got a phone call from Marlon to say that Mahmoud hadn't picked him up from school and suddenly I knew. I felt sick in my stomach. I knew he had done it.

I rang William in a complete state. He was very good in a crisis, very calm and collected. He told me to stay where I was, and he got there straight away. We jumped in a taxi and went to Marlon's school to pick him up, then we went to Khalid's school and got him. He goes to the same school as Allawi and Amira, a nice Victorian building in Maida Vale with mostly children of Middle Eastern parents. One of the teachers was still there, and she told me that Allawi and Amira hadn't turned up at school that day. I felt frantic with worry. How could I have let this happen? I was always warning other mums to watch out for the danger signs, and how they must always be alert and on guard. Now, like a fool, I had let it happen to me.

I phoned the Eastman Dental Hospital and the receptionist told me that no one had turned up for Amira's appointment. Then William called the police. I was aware of the commotion around me, but I wasn't taking it in; it didn't seem in any way real to me. I felt as though this was all wrong, this could not be happening. It was too shocking to absorb. And with all the missions that I had carried out for other mums, this was too cruel a trick of fate.

I was in a daze. How do you feel when the person you trust, whom you believe to be a good person, who supports you when you're helping other mothers in this situation, turns around and steals your kids? How would you feel? Distraught is not even close. In the space of an hour, my whole world had caved in.

It's the most horrible emotion a mother can ever imagine having to feel. I kept looking out the window every time I heard a car. I drove around in the taxi, back and forwards from the flat to the station, looking out for them, hoping against hope I would see them, that there'd be some reason for it. It was an absolute nightmare. Khalid was inconsolable and Marlon was also in a terrible state. My sister phoned and Mahmoud's sister, Ibtihal, turned up. I just kept smelling their clothes, looking around for things that Mahmoud had taken. The police were at the house until eleven o'clock that night, then in the morning they came back and said that Mahmoud had taken a flight to Beirut the previous morning; the airport police had confirmed it.

They told us that, had they still been in Lebanon, the Lebanese Government could have intervened and returned the children, but that there was a record of Mahmoud crossing the border into Syria and there was nothing that could be done. Apparently, the British Foreign Office held the view that, if they were in Lebanon, there were people who could get them back, that the authorities there would be helpful. But not in Syria.

On the day he took them, I was devastated – but I was livid as well. I honestly believe if I could have gotten hold of Mahmoud and a gun, I would have killed him. I would have blown his head off. I can remember around that time William being with me, trying to keep things ticking over, and lots of people coming in and out of the flat, but I didn't really pay attention to what was going on. I was too distraught. I was sitting by the window looking out, waiting for them to come back, but knowing in my heart of hearts they weren't coming.

I didn't even have keys to get into the flat, as Mahmoud had borrowed my set that morning, so I had to get a spare set from my friend Fatima. I will never ever forgive Mahmoud for what he put me through. I now know that he told the little ones that Mummy knew all about it, that she was going to follow them and meet them out there, all this bullshit. We were going to meet up in Iraq. In Iraq! I mean, there was a war going on there, in case he hadn't noticed. But he told them all this to get them on the plane.

Ibtihal stayed at the flat throughout the evening. Despite my role in helping her to come to the UK, and the fact that I had risked imprisonment to get her son Yussuf back, there was no great love lost between us. I had found her to be cold and calculating, only ever doing things out of self-interest. She arrived with nothing, now she has a council house paid for with housing benefit, she has an income from social security, she's going to university . . . And she's never really acknowledged the fact that we gave her financial support when she first arrived in the UK.

She told me that Mahmoud had been to see her a few days before and had asked for money because he wanted to take the children to Iraq. She said that he wanted to leave with the children because he wasn't happy that I had asked him for a divorce, and he didn't want to stay because I had told him that I wanted to take the children to America. I could see how this might have come about. I had told him that things weren't working out, that I couldn't live like this any longer. We weren't getting on and I needed to think about the future. There was constant arguing and stress; it was just awful, as anyone in an unhappy relationship can testify. It wasn't fair on the kids. During yet another row I had lost my temper and shouted that I wanted a divorce, but I don't know where he got the idea that I was planning to move to the States with the kids. Then there was William. Although it was a platonic friendship, seeing me spend so much time with another man must have upset Mahmoud's male pride. To him, whether or not we were having an affair – and we weren't – may have been immaterial. He didn't like to see his wife associating with another man and especially not in front of his children. I can see that now. He may have put two and two together and made five, but my belief is that he was using him as an excuse to justify what he was planning to do. I had never said that I didn't love him any more, just that I couldn't take that way of living.

Later that evening, my sister Sandra turned up with her husband Paul. They were being really nice and supportive, until she dropped her bombshell. She said that Ibtihal had called her the night before to say that Mahmoud was talking about planning to take the children. I couldn't believe what I was hearing. How could she not have told me? She protested that she had called Mahmoud to challenge him, but he was out, or his phone was switched off, and he never returned the call. I was livid. Had she called me, I would have been alert and on my guard, and that bit of information could have stopped my kids from going.

Sandra didn't seem to understand why I was so upset when I learned that she'd had some sort of warning about what was going to happen. She was serenity itself, saying that it was all going to be fine, that I shouldn't worry. Well, it wasn't going to be fine – my kids had been taken. It really annoyed me – Mahmoud had phoned Ibtihal and that should have set off alarm bells, but she didn't think it was necessary to tell me.

But back on Tuesday, 25 March, as I went to the house with William, it was all a bit of a daze. With Sandra turning up, Ibtihal, the world and his wife, I couldn't think straight. My flat felt like

Piccadilly Circus. When the police came round and confirmed that he had flown to Beirut that day, I checked for passports and they were still there. It was only the next day that the police told me they had new passports. They had been issued on 17 January, two months earlier, so he had been planning it for some time. He had gone behind my back when I was in Iran helping another mum and sorted out duplicate British passports. He'd said the originals were lost and they needed new ones. He'd got our GP to sign the backs of the photos. It was all premeditated. That's what really hurts. All that time I was blissfully unaware of what was coming. How could I ever trust him again?

He had started taking clothes slowly, little by little. He must have been storing them at a friend's house. I later found out that he had been at a woman's house – let's call her Leila. She must have been helping him. She's someone who used to like Mahmoud before we were married. She's Iraqi, from Baghdad. To this day, I can't forgive her – as a mother, if she had any idea where my kids were, or what was going to happen, she should have told me.

I didn't have her number, but later on I paid someone to get his mobile-phone records so I could try to trace him. It can be done, but it's expensive because it's illegal. I paid a private detective about £1,500 to get this information. Mahmoud had phoned Leila after he had left, so I knew she was in on it.

I learned later that, after he flew to Beirut, he crossed into Syria the next day. The kids told me that they went up into the mountains and stayed somewhere with a family who had a dog and they had to sleep on the floor. To this day, he refuses to tell me who these people were in case I try to do anything to them. I don't know what he thinks I would do, but there you go.

Interpol were able to tell us that there was a record of him crossing the Syrian border, but I knew that he was in Syria because when I tried to ring his mobile, it was connecting to SyriaTel. I would ring and leave a message or text him, begging him to at least let me speak to the children, but at the time he was so cold-hearted he never took the calls nor rang me back. What hurt was that he had phoned Sandra and Paul a couple of times. They said Mahmoud had told them I couldn't talk to the children and that he was taking them home to Najaf. Najaf! In the middle of a war! And all this time, I was watching the conflict unravel on the news.

At 11.30 a.m. on 26 March, two US cruise missiles slammed into a central marketplace crowded with shoppers and motorists in the populated neighbourhood of Al-Shaab in northern Baghdad. At least 15 innocent civilians were killed and over 50 injured. A news report on Al-Jazeerah showed charred cars and at least one blood-stained body being carried away. Reports of unrest were filtering through and I found the images of children with bandages hard to bear. Reports were describing the lives of those hurt or killed in the attack: unsuspecting Iraqis preparing lunch for customers in the market one minute, their livelihoods devastated the next. One article I read at the time in *The Guardian* really made me afraid for my children: 'home isn't safe, the farms are not safe, the market isn't safe. *Nowhere is safe.*'

Add to all this the nightly images of Baghdad having the crap bombed out of it, the night sky lit up with explosions and tracer fire, and you can imagine I was going out of my mind. Although Mahmoud's family live in Najaf, which is about 90 miles south of Baghdad, his brother lives in the capital. I didn't know whether he was crazy enough to go there, but he had been crazy enough to take the kids to a war zone, so anything was possible. And even Najaf was dangerous. Militiamen loyal to Shia cleric Moqtada Sadr were based there, so the city was going to be a hot spot.

Reading about these attacks, I was frantic. The idea that they could have been among the dead, lying in a pile of rubble, was too awful to contemplate. William was trying to convince me that the kids would be all right, but how could he know? Talk of precision bombing is rubbish. In a war situation, thousands of civilians are killed.

It was actually on the day that Baghdad was liberated that

Mahmoud finally crossed into Iraq. I remember watching the incredible scenes on TV that day, as Saddam's statue was pulled down.

He called Sandra from Syria and told her the kids were fine, but that they weren't coming back. At least then I knew what his intentions were and that I would have to go after them. I didn't know what I was going to do when I got there, I just knew I had to go.

Chapter 10

All Roads Lead to Nowhere

The night I realised the kids had gone, I decided to call Monica from Shine. I knew from my experiences that being out in the Middle East – staying in hotels, paying drivers and fixers and so on – took a lot of money. I thought if I could somehow get them to consider doing another film, this time about me, they would surely cover the expenses. She came round the next day with Michelle and a lady called Ros from Channel 4.

That week was crazy – everyone was visiting with food and to see how they could help. That's one of the great things about the tight-knit community I live in: everyone rallies round. I have a good friend called Latifa, whose son plays with Marlon, and she slept on the sofa that night while I sat up in the armchair. I was grateful to have her company in that dark hour.

When Monica and Michelle turned up, Latifa left us to it – it was time to get down to business. I sat at the table with them, and it was like a council of war. Thank God they were around because I was too distraught to think straight. The one thing we were all agreed on was that we had to get out to Syria to try to find them before the madman tried to take them into Iraq – if he hadn't done so already.

Monica was very practical and took control of the situation. She pointed out that it was going to be expensive flying out to the Middle East, hiring drivers and paying fixers . . . we'd done it before with Alison Lalic, so we knew what was involved.

'Right, let's do what we can to raise funds,' she said enthusiastically. I told her that I would do anything; they could film it for a documentary again, anything to get my kids back. She told me not to worry, that she would take care of things. She kept her word. Paul Hamann, the creative director of Shine, was also amazing. I have a lot to be thankful to them for. I remember Paul being really strong, telling me not to worry, that we were going to get the kids back. The way he said it, I believed him.

William didn't like them, though; he was suspicious of them. He's a journalist himself, and he was questioning their motives. He was saying things like, 'Be careful of them, they don't care about you, they're using you, all they care about is the film.' He was personally involved and maybe he was being a little too protective. I was numb with shock and William was determined to look after me. I wasn't eating or drinking at that time.

So, Monica and Michelle helped to raise some money, I took all of mine, and between us we scraped some finance together. Everyone was very good to me. The help was incredible. I'll never forget it. Finally, on Tuesday, 1 April, we were ready to go.

People were advising me to be strong, to be detached, almost to treat it as though it was a job for one of my mums, but, of course, I couldn't. It's entirely different when it's your own children. I had been able to be strong for my mums when I had gone with them, but now it was my kids it was a different story. I'd gone from being the organiser to being the victim, and that was a new and disorientating role for me. I was only grateful that I had such good people around me, people that I could trust and who knew what they were doing.

I went down to Heathrow that afternoon with Monica, Michelle, Marlon and Khalid. I couldn't think straight – my cheeks were burning, I felt numb. I was also worried about money – we had a budget to work to, so we would have to be careful. And the kids were confused.

We soon boarded the plane and were off. It's not a long flight, only around four hours, but we were all very solemn; it was as though someone had died. I had done this so many times, but the familiarity of the routine was not at all comforting. It just felt like a horrible dream, and the atmosphere was deadly serious.

Monica and Michelle were being so good to the kids. Khalid was unsettled, so Monica bought him a British Airways teddy bear when the air hostesses came round with the trolley. He called it Brit and he still has it to this day. Monica gave him a hug and a cuddle, and I must say the boys were brilliant. As we were making our descent into Beirut, Khalid looked out of the window at the myriad twinkling lights below. He turned to me and said in a sad voice, 'Mummy, look at that enormous city. All those lights, all those people. How are we going to find Amira and Allawi?' The enormity of what we were doing hit me like a wall. I just felt like crying at the hopelessness of the situation. But I had to remain strong for the children.

I smiled at him and gave his hand a squeeze. 'Don't worry, darling. We'll find them, don't you worry about that.' I wished I felt as optimistic as I sounded.

Whalid, a driver I had used on previous trips to Beirut, met us at the airport. He is a lovely man and I am still in touch with him. He took us to where we were staying, a place called the Savoy Suites Hotel. It's a beautiful modern block of apartments just ten minutes' drive from the airport. They are beautifully furnished, so it's like being in a lovely flat. It was better than a hotel, as it wasn't so strange for the children. They liked it there, not least because there was a Burger King opposite and, of course, a beach. It was beautiful, with lovely Arabic blankets on the beds. We checked in and put the kids to bed. We were all exhausted, so we had an early night. I even managed to sleep.

The next morning, we sat down and planned what we were going to do. We headed out of the hotel and walked along the main road by the beach. It was a lovely day, the sun was shining and Beirut looked wonderful. The traffic was incredible, really busy. Monica had arranged a fixer in Beirut, a lady named Lena, who had organised a driver for us, so the first thing to do was go and see her.

Lena is a single mum of two and lives in a gorgeous flat in Beirut. She's also a journalist. She told me later that I was like a 50-year-old woman when she met me that day, with no life left in me. She was the one who had been able to find out what time Mahmoud had crossed the border and all those kinds of details. Her boyfriend was the chief of police in Beirut, so her contacts were incredible. We're still in touch; she's been over to see us.

So, we arrived at the block of flats where Lena lived; her VW Beetle was outside. It had a huge pair of furry dice hanging from the rear-view mirror, so I knew she had a sense of humour and that we would hit it off. She lived in a penthouse apartment and I remember the lift wasn't working, so we had to take the stairs. A little Filipino lady opened the door.

Lena had a big, fluffy, two-tone Persian cat, which I adored – I've got two cats of my own – and Khalid started playing with it. She told him her two girls were out skiing and Khalid's eyes opened wide in surprise. 'In Beirut, you can ski in the morning and swim in the sea in the afternoon,' she laughed. He was fascinated. She was very kind to him. When the girls came in a little later, they took my boys off to play on the Internet, and the rest of us sat down and had tea. It was time to get our plan together.

Lena said she was prepared to come into Iraq with us if need be, but I told her I didn't think that would be necessary. Our best information was that Mahmoud and the kids were in Syria and, despite my fears the week before, in my heart of hearts I didn't think he would be so foolish as to go to Iraq while the war continued. Sandra said that he had told her he was going there, but

I didn't believe it. No father would be so crazy as to do that. You'd have to be demented or senile, and no matter how screwed up Mahmoud had obviously become, I didn't think even he would go somewhere that was being bombed. So we agreed that our first point of attack would have to be Syria.

Whalid suggested driving us to Damascus, the capital of Syria, to see if we could pick up any leads. He would take us to the border and we could change cars there – Lena, who was coming with us, would organise a driver on the other side of the border.

The road from Beirut to the Lebanon–Syria border follows one of the most well-known ancient routes of the East, passing Dahr El Baidar mountain and ending at Al Massnaa. We had a short stop at one of the cafés in Chtaura on the Lebanese side, where we changed drivers. The drive from Beirut to Damascus is about three hours in all, but because people were very worried about the war, there were lots of checkpoints.

It's a lovely drive down through hills and mountains, though. You can see Damascus all laid out, spreading below you. I looked at all these buildings and thought, 'My kids could be down there somewhere and I wouldn't even know.'

The driver stopped just before Damascus, where there's a huge duty-free shopping centre with lots of names that you would recognise, like Dunkin' Donuts, and we had a coffee and got water for the kids. They were so tired, they weren't interested. We were all quiet, as though the seriousness of what were doing had taken over. I was praying that we would be successful and every so often one of the boys would take hold of my hand and give it a squeeze, as if to reassure me that it was all going to be OK.

We arrived at a small family hotel. There were a lot of Iraqis there, presumably wanting to be somewhere safe away from the war. No one paid us much attention – they were probably so used to the media that they thought we were a film crew, what with Monica's camera, and they left us alone. Normally, when you've got drivers and fixers and cameras, you stand out like a sore thumb. I was in a room with the boys with a couple of single beds that we pushed together. I remember Khalid and Marlon were really tired and it was so hot; they just wanted to go and play football in the park after being cooped up in the car for so long, but by now it was late afternoon and we needed to think about having a good evening meal and getting some rest. We would have a lot to do the next day.

After dinner, I gave them a shower and got them changed into their pyjamas. We looked out of the window at this strange city. We could hear the *adhan* from a nearby mosque calling people to prayer. It was really dusty and really a miserable part of the city, with blocks of flats opposite. It was dowdy and depressing, and I felt quite down. It wasn't like the Marriott or the sort of hotel that I was used to, so it wasn't really helping my mood. Damascus was packed full of people and I just thought, 'What am I doing here?'

I climbed into bed, cuddled up to the boys and fell asleep. We slept well that night. The next morning, I was woken about 6 a.m. by the *adhan*. It makes you so aware that you're in another part of the world. The boys couldn't believe it, they jumped out of bed, all excited. We got ready, went downstairs and saw Monica and Michelle, and found our way to the local police station.

There was a young policeman on duty from the town of Aleppo, who couldn't have been friendlier. I told him that my husband and kids had gone missing, and that I wanted them registered as such in case someone saw them, you never know. He was so helpful. I was not to worry, he said, they would do everything they could to find them. Even though I didn't think there would be anything they could do, it was encouraging just to see a friendly face. I was really grateful that he was kind to me.

The next thing to think about was trying to get visas to get into Iraq, so we went to the Iraqi Embassy. I told the kids in advance that, if anyone asked, they were to say we had been on holiday with Mahmoud and had somehow got split up.

The funny thing was that the Iraqi Embassy was directly

opposite the American Embassy. A few hundred miles away, one country was bombing the living daylights out of the other, yet here in Damascus, both embassies were open for business and tolerated the existence of each other. They could even have their embassies opposite each other and carry out the formalities of state business as though nothing had changed. Mind you, there was a lot of security outside.

It was chaos at the embassy; it was heaving with people who were there to get visas or try to get information about relatives. All the men were sitting on one side and the women on the other. Outside, children in school uniform were demonstrating against the Americans. It was madness: a world in upheaval. My heart sank. With all these thousands of people caught up in the consequences of war, uprooted from their homes and displaced, how would we find my children?

So, there I was, going into the embassy with a British passport – they hated the British because of the war – I thought I had no chance. Eventually, the ambassador's secretary came out. His name was Tahir and he was a lovely man, about 5 ft 9 in., bald with gold-rimmed Cartier glasses, dressed in a suit and tie. I think he took a bit of a shine to me. I was being a bit flirty, smiling a lot. I had found in previous missions that if I could get men on my side in this area of the world, it could make life a lot easier. He organised drinks for the children and tea for us, then invited us into his office, sat down and asked what he could do for me. I explained that I had lost my husband. He thought I meant that he had died, and he offered his condolences. So I explained I meant that I had mislaid him, which he found amusing, given his misunderstanding. He asked if he was in Iraq, and I told him that I didn't know and that was why I was here, to see whether he had been in for a visa. He wouldn't have suspected that Mahmoud had abducted Allawi and Amira because I had the other two children with me. What man would take two children and not the other two? Of course, Mahmoud had known he could only persuade the younger two to leave without their mother; Marlon and Khalid would have asked too many questions.

I told him I wanted a visa to go into Iraq to see whether they were there. He told me that I would have to see the ambassador and went off. When he came back, he asked me to follow him. The ambassador was a short, stubby man with a moustache and glasses; a very nice man. He asked me whether I spoke Arabic and I told him that I did. He asked me why I wanted to go to Iraq and I told him that I was Iraqi, that my husband was Iraqi and we wanted to be reunited, that I thought Mahmoud would have gone to his mother's when we got separated. I don't know whether he believed my story or not, but he was maybe too polite to question me.

He started to tell us how dangerous it was in Iraq and that it would be impossible to get a visa that day. I told him that I didn't need one today, that I was going to carry on looking for them in Syria, then I would go to Iraq. Then he asked me if there were problems between me and my husband. I laughed as though it was a ridiculous idea.

'What, me and Mahmoud? No, of course not. We've been married a long time, there's no problem.'

He thought about it and said, 'OK, we will do a visa for you and your children.'

I asked about Michelle, who was also with us. Monica had waited outside because of her blonde hair and American passport.

'No, I am afraid that is impossible,' he said. I asked him why and he responded that she could go as a human shield. This meant that he would not issue a normal visa, but would approve her entry to the country if she joined one of the official convoys of Western pacifists, or 'human shields' as they were referred to in the press, heading into Iraq.

We weren't going to agree to that, although Michelle said she would do it if necessary. That's what I love about the people at Shine, they're so full of positive thinking; they can get things done when other people would give up.

We took the visas for me and the kids. I was so happy to have them because I was worried that Mahmoud could turn up and instruct them not to give me a visa – if the husband says so, his word goes. Because we had got there first, we were OK. We had them whatever happened. My elation soon turned to despair once again, though, when I considered the pitifully short amount of time this visa was offering me. Three days? My heart sank. I knew deep down that nothing would happen in just three days. We left the embassy and went back to the hotel.

The kids were tired again so I took them to a park so they could play football. It was a funny little park: there was no greenery and it was all dusty with shrubs. I sat and watched and had some Arabic tea. There were lots of romantic couples walking hand-in-hand, and you could tell they were newlyweds. There were lots of children playing. The driver who had taken us from the Lebanese border down to Damascus came and joined us, and they played a bit of basketball together, which was good for the boys. It was nice for them to play, but I could tell they weren't putting their hearts into it. They kept looking over at me, as though to acknowledge my concern, as if to say, 'Don't worry, Mum, we're still here.' What a burden to have put on two kids' shoulders, to have their mum sitting there distraught on a bench in a strange city. I was anxious, in tears, wanting to know where my other kids were. But I had to keep focused and strong for Marlon and Khalid.

I felt guilty, like I should be doing something, out walking the streets looking for my kids. For all I knew, they were in Damascus. I looked at all the people walking past and thought, 'They could be walking down the street, on the other side of the road, and I wouldn't even know.' Everything goes through your head. It's like sitting in a waiting room at the doctor's wondering about each person's complaint. It's very weird to be in a predicament like that, to be in a situation where your kids could be within earshot and you don't know. It's like once, when I was a child, I was at a market and got split up from my mum. I was panicking, wondering where she was.

And then I started wondering about the kids: what was going through their minds? Were they missing me? Did they have any idea what was going on? Was Mahmoud coping with Allawi, because he's a real handful. People kept telling me not to worry, that he would phone because Allawi would be driving him mad, but that was the worst thing – I did think he would phone, but he never did. We kept trying to ring him, but could never get through – his mobile was always switched off.

We wandered around, looking everywhere, and, eventually, after a couple of days, Monica took me to one side and said, 'Look, Donya, it's not working. We need to go back now.' I think they were fed up. I don't think they'd had the heart to tell me that it was time to give up and go home. We'd just wandered around aimlessly, going into shops, cafés, whatever, with pictures of the kids, asking if anyone had seen them. And, of course, no one had. But it was time to be realistic. The kids had to go back to school. I didn't really know what I was doing.

'It's better if we go home and try to find another angle,' Monica was saying. 'We'll work on it. We need to find some leads. Just being out here is not achieving anything. We don't even know that they're in Syria, let alone Damascus. Let's go home and think about our next move. Maybe he'll phone, maybe we can trace the call. Anything is better than this.'

It was a lot of maybes. I felt empty, desolate, helpless.

Chapter 11

False Trails and Empty Promises

So that's what we did; we flew back from Beirut on Sunday, 6 April 2003.

On the Monday, I went to Kilburn, in north-west London, to look for dresses for Amira, as if to tell myself she was going to come back, that all of this was a terrible nightmare from which I would soon awake. While I was out, my mobile rang. It was Andrew Crofts, the writer who had helped with my first book. 'Look, Donya, this guy has been to see me about doing a book. He's a private detective – he claims to be the best in England.'

I said to Andrew that he could give this guy my number and, sure enough, he rang. He said that he wanted to meet me, that he could help me get my children back. Of course, I was so desperate I would take any help I could get. He asked me where I lived and said he would be with me in a couple of hours. My God, I thought, he's keen.

He turned up at my flat that afternoon, and my first impressions weren't that good, to be honest. He was overweight, and I remember thinking he had great big feet. He drove a dark-coloured 4x4, and when he came in, he sat on the sofa and promised the kids that he would get them football shirts – which he never did. He claimed that he was in with some Premiership footballers, making all the right noises, telling them what they wanted to hear. I can get some signed football shirts for you from the top players, he said, and don't you worry about a thing, Marlon, I'm going to get your brother and sister back for you. I felt it was wrong, raising their hopes like that, building up their trust. Maybe he was a nice guy underneath, but he shouldn't have promised things that he couldn't deliver. He kept telling me not to worry, that he could do it, he had lots of contacts. It wasn't Andrew's fault, I hasten to point out, he'd only met him once.

One thing the detective did do was get Mahmoud's phone records for me. He said it would cost money, and it did – around £1,500. But at least he got them, which was one thing that he did manage to do, to give him his due. On the Tuesday, he came round to collect the money, then returned later with the records. He then said he was going to go down to Maroush, the restaurant where Mahmoud had worked, to enquire about calls that had been made the day he had left with the children. Mahmoud's colleagues there denied all knowledge of his plan to abduct Allawi and Amira, saying that he had told them he was going home to see his family. He had handed in his notice a couple of weeks before, so, looking back, there must have been days when he told me he was going to work and he wasn't – he was probably making last-minute arrangements for the trip.

When I looked at the phone records, I could see that he had called Leila and a man I'll call Hamada, another waiter at Maroush. We called them, but they denied all knowledge. I could see from the records that he had phoned Leila an hour before he took the kids, but she said she hadn't heard from Mahmoud in months and she didn't know anything about what he was up to.

'You're lying! I've got phone records here that prove you've been in touch,' I said. She tried to bluster her way through, saying she wouldn't do anything like that, so help her God; that she would do anything to help me get my children back; that it was nothing to do with them, and she would not get involved in a terrible thing like that. 'I'm a mother myself,' she said, 'I wouldn't inflict this suffering on another mother.'

I let her finish what she had to say and said, 'Don't lie to me. I know how you feel about Mahmoud. I'm a woman and I know when another woman fancies my husband.' I told her the whole community knew it, and carried on, saying, 'Look, whatever you think you know, don't tell lies for Mahmoud. What he has done is a very bad thing; I don't care what he has told you about me, I am a good mother. At least I don't throw myself at other men when they're married and I'm married as well.' And with that I put the phone down.

I got the same reception from Hamada. He was very polite but firm, and denied all knowledge. I said that if I found out he was lying, I would come after him. Of course, I knew he was lying. After some persuasion, he eventually gave in and admitted that they had been to his flat, that it was there that Mahmoud had changed them out of their school uniforms into casual clothes.

Throughout this period, I was keeping in touch with the police. At the time, there was a fantastic child-protection team run by a guy called Andy Mountfield based at Paddington Green. That team was so good to me, they could not have been kinder. But they were limited in what they could do once kids had been taken out of the country. A couple of them said, 'I wish we could just get on a plane and get your kids back, love,' but it's out of their jurisdiction; their hands are tied. The police were there the night the kids went missing and Andy would ring on a regular basis, asking whether there was any news.

Andy Mountfield is a lovely man, a dad in his 40s. Very dignified, very polite, very calm. He was like a doctor, the way he would speak to you and calm you down, set your mind at rest. Of course, he was a policeman, so he had to be very careful that all the advice he gave was within the bounds of the law. But he was very honest. And he was worried about the well-being of the children going into Iraq. He knew it was no place to take kids. He was always very professional, never crossed the line, but he made it clear that he was worried about them. He knew my background, how I had helped other mums; I think he always knew I was going to go after them. I think he accepted that and in his own way respected my position. Being involved in child protection, he was also worried about the welfare of Marlon and Khalid.

Later, when the kids came back, he came with his colleague, Margaret, to see us, and the difference in his facial expression and demeanour between when it was just me and when the kids were there was enormous. You could see how his face lit up. This is a man who loves kids – he's in the right job. All the encouragement and support he gave me was because he cared about the welfare of my children.

I think the police can say different things in different situations to assure you that everything is in hand and it's going to be all right, but when my kids went missing, I knew their limitations and how little they could do for me. I'd seen it too many times.

But the police – I mean here the ordinary police, as opposed to Andy Mountfield's child-protection unit – were slow to act. Because of my background, I know how imperative it is to act quickly, while there's even a remote chance of stopping a father with a child getting out of the country, and certainly to pick up the trail at the other end while it is still warm. But the police don't have that experience, that sense of urgency. William and I were ringing them, hassling them, and that's why they got on with it.

William was a great support. He was around the whole time, hugging me, fussing over me, making me eat, making me sleep. He would sleep in his own place but be back the next day. But I was so upset with everything that had happened, I even took it out on him, saying maybe it was because of him it had happened. Maybe Mahmoud was jealous and wanted to punish me. But William took it all and said, no, it would have happened anyway, pointing out that when Mahmoud had applied for the passports back in January I hadn't even met him. And he was right. He is a very good man. I often think about how I lashed out at him at that time, and how awful it is that, when we are unhappy, we hurt the ones we care about the most.

The private detective I'd hired announced we were going to Damascus on Wednesday, 9 April, two days after I'd met him. It was essential to move quickly while we could still trace Mahmoud's steps. He had a lead to say that Mahmoud had been using an Internet café in the Syrian capital, and he needed money for our plane fares. I rang Sandra and Paul – I didn't know who else to turn to. He said he had already paid for the tickets on his credit card, so he needed reimbursing. He also said that we'd need more money for drivers, hotels, everything else. All in all, he said we had to raise £2,000. He claimed he didn't need his own expenses, that he was working for free because he wanted to help, but he needed to cover the costs of the flights and also pay off contacts who were giving him these leads.

Looking back, it didn't really add up. I mean, tickets to Beirut can be as cheap as £250 and you certainly shouldn't pay more than £400 for one. I don't know why we needed all that money. But I wasn't thinking straight. I had lost my usual objectivity. I was just letting myself believe him, that he was going to get my kids back for me. He said that he would provide receipts for his expenses and return whatever wasn't used. It would all be legitimate and above board. To this day, he hasn't returned the unused money or accounted for his expenses.

That day, we drove up to meet Sandra and Paul on the motorway near their home in Stevenage. They were going to look after Khalid and Marlon while I was away, so I said goodbye to the kids and gave him the money they had lent me. Altogether, he was given about £3,000.

That night, I was on my own for the first time since the children had been taken. It was strange. I was very confused; I didn't know whom to trust. I thought everyone was lying to me, everyone had known what was going to happen, I was the last to know – I no longer felt that I could trust the community in which I lived, in which my children went to school. I knew that Mahmoud had confided in people – Hamada, Leila – so I thought he must also have confided in others whom I knew. Whom could I trust? That really hurt.

On the Wednesday afternoon, we flew out to Beirut. As we were checking in, a lovely woman named Sandra, who worked for the airline, said that she recognised me and knew my story, and she upgraded us. We told her that we were going to Iraq – I didn't want to tell her the real reason, so I told her we were doing a project for charity, to try to raise money to help my mums. I had a great rest on that flight. We arrived in Beirut late at night, about 10.30 p.m., and expected to be met by Whalid again, but there was no sign of him. Once we called him, though, he came and drove us to the border, where we had to change drivers before the onward journey to Damascus. I was worried sick about Khalid and Marlon, but I was being pushed on by an inner force. We got to the hotel, the same place I had stayed on the previous trip, at about 1.30 a.m. I remember it felt very cold. I went straight to bed and fell asleep, dreaming of the children.

In the morning, the *adhan* woke me, so I was up early. We had breakfast and then we went out looking. The day was heating up. I recall there was a dog that seemed to come out of nowhere which jumped up at us – it was taller than the detective when it was on its hind legs. It gave me a real shock, but I suppose it was just being inquisitive. Who could blame it? He stood out quite a lot: a burly, Western guy, built like an outhouse with combat trousers tucked into his boots. He looked like he was my bodyguard.

We walked around the city centre all day, same as before, on a wild-goose chase, looking for Mahmoud and the kids, asking in bars and cafés. We went to the Internet café, but they couldn't tell us anything. Then he said he had information that they'd been seen in a flat near the café, so we started knocking on people's doors, showing them photos, asking if they had seen them. But, of course, they hadn't. It was all to no avail.

One funny thing did happen to me, though – I met one of Mahmoud's friends walking in the street there in Damascus. His name also happens to be Mahmoud. I asked whether he had seen the kids, but he said he hadn't. I didn't tell him my business, we just chatted for a minute, then he asked me to mention him to Mahmoud and he was on his way. By now, I was growing suspicious about how helpful this private detective was going to be. 'Well, you told me that you could find Mahmoud for me, and you did – unfortunately, it's the wrong one,' I quipped.

At 6 p.m., we went back to the hotel. He was sweating by the bucketload; the heat was too much for him, especially with his excess weight. He was on the phone to his wife. I wasn't eavesdropping, but I could tell he was getting grief from her. She was expecting their baby. I went to his room and asked what we should do now.

'Look, Donya, I think we should go home. We're not going to find them.'

I was flabbergasted. 'What do you mean?'

'I've spoken to my contacts and I've been given information that they're no longer in Damascus. What I think we should do is to go back home, have a meeting with Paul Hamann and the Shine people, and see whether we can get a proper amount of money together to do this thing. We can get them to film us, make a documentary, and we'll all get some money out of it. Think how great it would be if we could get it on film when we find the kids and bring them back home!'

It was as though he was writing the script for a film in his own mind, with him cast as a Bruce Willis-type hero at the centre of it. I knew that Monica and the people at Shine would see through him. Michelle is very shrewd and quite hard-nosed; she's a producer and her boyfriend is a journalist, so no one could pull the wool over her eyes. I grew cold. I could see now that he was only in it for money and glory.

'Listen, it doesn't work that way. These are my kids we're talking about. If anyone's bringing them home, it's me.'

So we abandoned the mission. For me, it was the second time in one week. I felt very flat. We flew back to London again via Beirut. When we got to Heathrow, we were waiting for our luggage and his wife rang. They were obviously having a row; I could tell she was shouting at him. He came off the phone, gave me a rueful shrug and said, 'She's left me.' As though I had the time and energy to be thinking about his problems. I believe they'd had a row while we were in Damascus and that was the real reason we had to come back.

Looking back, to be fair to him, he got me Mahmoud's phone records. But all this talk of sightings and contacts was baloney. I don't think he had any more information than we did. I think his plan was to stay out there and see what we could find, but he hadn't anticipated the trouble he was going to be in with his wife. With the problems he was having, he couldn't concentrate on the work he was supposed to be doing with me. He disappeared and I got a taxi back home.

On the way, I phoned Marlon, who was anxious to hear news. I had to tell him I hadn't found them but reassured him with, 'Don't worry, darling, I will.' They were getting used to that.

When I got home, Tracey was with the kids. Marlon was lying on the sofa. It turned out that he'd had to go to the hospital because of a problem with his foot. I felt terrible; I was in tears. They'd spent the first night with Sandra and Paul, then Tracey had brought them back home. I felt that as well as not being allowed to be a mother to my missing kids, I was being a bad mother to the ones at home.

Chapter 12

Getting Mad, Getting Even

One morning, about a week after I got back from my second trip, I woke up sitting in the armchair where I'd fallen asleep the night before. I'd spent many nights in that armchair. On a whim, I dialled Mahmoud's number. He answered. He wouldn't tell me where he was, but SyriaTel flashed on my screen. As they had started operating in Iraq, I couldn't be certain whether he was there or still in Syria – I would later find out that he was by then in Iraq. Lena had put up posters in Damascus with pictures of the kids in case anyone had seen them, offering a reward, but there was no news so it had seemed unlikely they were still there.

I knew now that the only person who could get my kids back was me. As ever, money was the problem. Where could I get it from? I got in touch once again with Sharon Hendry, the women's editor at *The Sun*, and she came to see me. She was a beautiful girl, very pretty, in her mid-30s. We've become good friends. She came round to my flat to discuss things with me and the next day came up with the goods – she came back with £8,000 and contracts to sign. It was to be an exclusive for *The Sun*, for the women's pages. 'You're very lucky,' she said. 'Everyone at Shine likes you so much. We all want you to succeed, to get your kids back.'

What prompted me to sell my story was that the journalist I'd spoken to earlier from a Sunday paper had been in touch again. He said that he knew that my kids had gone and he was threatening to run a story about it. He said it would be better for me to do an exclusive with him, but that he would run the story anyway without my help and I wouldn't get any money. I don't know how he knew – he claimed Mahmoud had rung him, trying to sell his story, but I didn't believe him. Mahmoud is not media-savvy; I don't think he would have had the first idea about how to go about doing that. Anyway, for what it's worth, subsequently Mahmoud has sworn blind that he never contacted anyone, and I actually believe him. The journalist was rather unpleasant, saying that the paper could do a story on the real Donya, how I was money-grabbing, manipulative and ruthless. That's how newspapers work – one minute you're Mother Teresa, the next you're the Whore of Babylon. You often hear people say how the papers love to build someone up only to destroy them – and now I was seeing it all first-hand.

Anyway, I received the money from *The Sun* and was ready to go. A number of friends within the community offered to come with me, but it would never have worked – their husbands would never have agreed to it. There was one lovely Tunisian girl called Souad, who really wanted to help. I went to her house and she cooked me a meal while we talked it through, but it was impossible – she had a baby. We had a joke about it, though, because Mahmoud had bumped into her car months before, and he was supposed to pay her £50 to cover the damage. We had a good laugh imagining her turning up wherever Mahmoud was hiding out with the kids and banging on the door. When he answered, she would say, 'I've come for my £50 – and while we're at it, she wants her kids back!' Sometimes laughing was the only way through.

A few days later, Tracey came round and I told her I was going to Iraq on my own to find the kids.

'You can't possibly go on your own!' she screeched.

'I haven't got much choice – unless you want to come with me?'

She looked at me and, after a minute, said, 'Yeah, OK, I'll come with you.'

I stared at her open-mouthed. She was still capable of surprising me after all these years. I could tell she wasn't joking – she wouldn't about something so serious. 'I'm buying my flight this afternoon,' I said. 'If you're serious, I'll buy a flight for you as well, but you won't be able to change your mind. If you say yes now, you're going to have to see it through.'

She said she was serious, so I went down to Queensway and bought our tickets from one of those chaotic travel agents' shops that seem the same from Bayswater to Beirut. When I came back later on, Tracey was there keeping an eye on the kids. I showed her the tickets and she couldn't believe it. The die was cast.

Tracey had been working in a Darby and Joan Club doing voluntary work. All the old ladies in Watford had been following the story, so they were incredibly excited when Tracey said she was going out to Iraq to get the kids. She came down the day before with her bags, and we started packing our belongings. I went up to Kilburn and bought three huge suitcases – I didn't know how long we would be away. I packed everything, not just for the boys, but clothes for Allawi and Amira as well. I made sure I'd done everything I was supposed to have done – paid all my bills, told the school and everyone else I could think of that we would be away for a short while – then I took one last look around the flat and pulled the door to and locked it. It was time to go. I told Andy Mountfield I was going and he just said, 'Godspeed.' He couldn't sanction what I was doing, of course – it was illegal – but he as good as wished me luck with it. He knew he couldn't stop me, nothing could have.

I spoke to Ibtihal before I left and she tried to talk me out of it. She said the kids would be well looked after by her mother, that I should wait for all the madness of the war to stop and for Mahmoud to come to his senses. But I told her I didn't care how dangerous it was,

Mahmoud should not have put me – or the kids – in this situation. If anything happened to us, even if it meant we all died, at least we would do so together. I asked her how her family could have let this happen to me, after everything I'd done for them all. 'I helped you get your son,' I said. They can't have appreciated it, otherwise how could they have stood by and let it happen? People are always so desperate, so grateful before you help them, but, afterwards, they seem to forget very quickly what you have done for them. 'I helped you, I fed you, I looked after you. I brought you and your two sons to England. And this is how you repay my kindness?'

'Don't blame me, Donya,' she replied. 'I cannot condone what Mahmoud has done – he has done a very bad thing. He is not my brother any longer.'

Fine words, but the fact was I believed she'd had foreknowledge of what Mahmoud had been planning and she hadn't seen fit to warn me. In my book, that made her a partner in crime, what lawyers might call an accessory before the fact. So, we fell out. It was just another casualty of what Mahmoud had done. There is so much damage, so much pain caused by the selfish and thoughtless actions of these fathers that the fallout can take years to settle.

Another worry that I had at this time, as if I didn't have enough on my plate, was that Andrew had finished my first book. I was getting phone calls from the publishers saying I wasn't pulling my weight, that I should be doing publicity to help promote the book. But how could I do the endless round of radio shows, daytime TV, magazine articles, talking about these mothers I had helped in the past, when my own husband had taken my kids? I was on the verge of a nervous breakdown – and the last thing on my mind was talking to the press and media about other mothers. Even if they said to me that by doing this promotion we can guarantee your book will be an international bestseller and you will make £1 million, it would have made no difference.

My friend Trish saw us off when the taxi came to take us to the airport. She was crying, telling us to take care of ourselves and get home safely. We waved goodbye and set off for Heathrow. By this stage it was mid-May, and almost eight weeks had passed since I had last seen my two youngest children.

Tracey, Marlon, Khalid and I all checked in for the afternoon flight to Beirut. My God, I thought, I do this as regularly as some people go to the supermarket. The flight was uneventful, and we arrived in Beirut on the Saturday night at about 10 p.m., as usual. This time, though, I felt different. I was not desperate, confused, chaotic. A kind of peace had settled over me – I knew why I was there and what I was going to do. It brought a sense of acceptance. One way or another, I would not be going home without my children.

On the previous two trips, the problem was that there was no plan, no mission. We were turning up like headless chickens in the hope that the kids would just present themselves. I had allowed other people to get involved, to obscure my thinking. Now, I had clarity; I knew exactly what I was doing.

Whalid met us at the airport. He was like a favourite uncle, with hugs, kisses and smiles for the children. He led us to his car, a new blue seven-seater – the height of luxury. He drove us straight to the Syrian border. Whalid went into the office with the passports and the paperwork, and he came out frowning. 'It's not good news.'

I was immediately worried. Perhaps somebody had informed the authorities of what I was planning and my name had been given to all the border guards with strict instructions not to let me through. As I have said before, it's a man's world in the Middle East. If these men had any idea that I – a liberated Western woman – was coming to their region to snatch children back from another man, I wouldn't have stood a chance.

I shouldn't have taken it so personally, though. The problem was that, apparently, Colin Powell, US Secretary of State at the time, had issued an edict that no Iraqi nationals were to be allowed into Syria. I tried to remonstrate, saying the kids had been in Syria only two weeks previously, but the guards shook their heads. The rule had just come into play and nothing could be done. They were very respectful, no doubt because I was wearing a hijab, but they were unmovable. The problem was the kids – although I had a British passport, they had Iraqi ones.

One took pity on me and said, 'Look, there is nothing we can do here – but if you want my advice, I would try to find another way across. Why don't you try Jordan?'

I got back in the car and told Tracey the news. We were unsure about our next step. We had been so charged up, planning to get straight across Syria and into Iraq, full of adrenalin, that now we'd hit a snag, we felt deflated. We decided the best thing we could do would be to go back to Beirut, get a good night's sleep and see what the next day brought. We rang the Savoy and, yes, there was a free apartment. Whalid turned the car around and we headed back the way we had come.

The next day, Whalid came back. It was time for a war summit. We went downstairs to a row of shops, where we had some breakfast. Sitting there in the sunshine with our coffee and pastries, it was hard to believe that we would be going into a war-torn country within a day or two. It seemed surreal, but there was no option.

We decided that it would be best to go on without the children. We could travel more quickly that way. The kids had their breakfast and seemed quite happy and content. 'Aunt Tracey and I have to go into Syria. You can stay with Uncle Whalid,' I said. They were happy with this arrangement; Whalid was good to them, and they felt safe with him.

'You come to my house and play with my children while your mummy goes to pick up your brother and sister,' Whalid said. He took the kids away, then he came back for us. It was time to go.

We set off for Syria using the same route as before: across the border and down the hills into the sprawl of Damascus. This time, we were focused – we went straight to the Iraqi Embassy to get visas which would allow us into Iraq. Without them, we would never get across the border. We couldn't believe it when we got there. Last time, the embassy had been practically besieged by scores of desperate people whose lives had been so sadly and severely disrupted, the flotsam and jetsam of war; now, it was closed. I had taken a bag of Iraqi sweets and a couple of small presents from the UK to give to Tahir, the lovely secretary to the ambassador who had been so helpful to us on the previous occasion, but there was no one around; the building was shut and shuttered.

A consequence of the overthrow of Saddam's Ba'ath Party and the immediate upshot for me was that all the emblems of a state, all its functions, had been suspended. And that included the embassy in Damascus. I wondered whether we should head to Jordan and see whether we could somehow manage to get across the border there. First, though, I decided to try knocking on the front door. To my surprise, the door was opened and I found myself nose to nose with a security guard. Who was paying his salary now was anybody's guess.

In broken English, he said, 'Nobody here, nobody work, all gone now.'

I recognised him from my previous visit, so I said hello in Arabic. I held out the sweets to him and he took one. In Arabic culture, it is a sign of respect to offer a stranger something to eat; it is a kind of universal peace offering.

He took one and said, 'I remember you, you lady who looking for her husband and her children. You find them?' I told him we had not found them, and indeed had been hoping that he might have been able to give us news of a sighting. It had been a long shot, but I had been hoping that Mahmoud would have come to the embassy to get visas and the necessary paperwork to cross the border back into Iraq with the children. I was forced to conclude ruefully that either he had crossed from somewhere else, was not in Iraq or had relied on his Iraqi passport to get him past the border guards.

I told the security man that my husband and children were in Iraq, and that I was going to meet them there. His eyes widened, and he shook his head. 'Impossible,' he said, shaking his head sadly.

'Why is it impossible?' I demanded to know.

'Impossible,' he said once more, reverting to his rudimentary English. 'No visas, embassy closed.'

'What about Tahir? Where is he? Is he still in Damascus?'

The man's face broke into a smile. At last, he could offer me something positive, and it clearly made him happy to be able to help a damsel in distress, even if it was such a small thing. 'No problem, I call Tahir. You wait, I come.' And with that he went back into the embassy.

He was as good as his word because ten minutes later a car drew up beside us and out jumped Tahir. He smiled and bowed slightly in recognition. I introduced Tracey to him and he suggested that we jump into the car; we would go to his flat where we could talk. Our driver followed us and waited outside. He had a beautiful apartment with a high ceiling and enormous windows. It was furnished in an Arabic style, naturally, with lots of gold fittings and furniture, ornate rugs and highly embroidered curtains. He called his maid, a Moroccan woman, and asked her to bring some tea. We sat at an enormous table in his front room and, after drinking some tea and making polite conversation, got down to business.

At the table where we were sitting, there were piles of paperwork and – most importantly – dozens of virgin Iraqi passports, which naturally caught my eye. I explained our predicament and asked whether we could buy Iraqi passports to ensure our safe passage across the border. He shook his head firmly, but politely. 'That I cannot do, Donya. But why do you need to do this anyway? What is wrong with the visas I issued you with last week when you came to the embassy?'

I told him that the visas had only been valid for three days, so they had expired. He sat and looked at me for a moment. He said he would see what he could do. After a few calls, he came back into the room with a smile. He had managed to secure a visa for me.

Then I realised we had another problem. My visa was fine now, but what was Tracey going to do? Tahir assured me that I was worrying unduly, that the border controls would not be as vigilant as I was expecting. He explained that when they stopped the car and saw my passport and visa, they would wave the car through. I was not convinced. Through my experiences of helping other women get their children back, I had been in situations at borders too many times for my liking, and it wasn't my experience that border guards were as happy-go-lucky and laid-back as Tahir imagined. Tracey spoke up and said she was willing to take the risk.

'But what if we get there and I get through and you get turned back? What will happen then?' I asked.

Tracey displayed the down-to-earth pragmatism that would prove to be so invaluable later on during this trip. 'Well, we'll worry about it if it happens. I'll get a driver to take me back to Beirut and wait for you there. It wouldn't be the end of the world.'

So, it was decided. We thanked Tahir for all his help and made our way back down to the car. As it was by now around 6 p.m., we agreed that we would head back to Beirut and cross into Iraq the next day. After meeting Whalid at the border again, we returned to the Savoy apartments, our regular home from home, and the next morning headed straight to the Jordanian Embassy. Despite Tahir's assurances that we would sail breezily through border control in Syria, I was not convinced. I couldn't feel this was a responsible and reliable course of action.

The embassy was at the top of a hill in a somewhat unattractive area. I remember there seemed to be dozens of stray cats milling about. The building itself was not at all imposing; it was a rather dusty, provincial affair with a few posters of King Hussein on the walls. Khalid was staring wide-eyed at the gun a soldier was carrying while standing on patrol at the entrance. In Britain, it is pretty rare to see guns, but in the Middle East they are everywhere, and it was a bit of a shock to him.

The soldier smiled at him, as if to reassure him, and nodded in a friendly manner, indicating that we should go in. I had phoned them before we left to explain that we wanted to get visas to cross into Iraq in order to meet up with my husband and children, now that the war was, in theory, over. I had been assured that it would not be a problem, that we could come and get them that very day. True to their word, when I had explained what we wanted, they issued the visas without any questions, and handed back our passports with a smile.

I couldn't believe how easy it was. Usually, you need to apply for a visa in the UK before you leave, or you can certainly expect to have to wait several days before you get anywhere. Simply to have them handed over like that was incredible. If the rest of the trip went as smoothly, I would have a lot to be thankful for.

Armed with our new visas, we headed straight to the airport. We couldn't expect Whalid to drive us along the route we would be taking now, so instead he took us to departures and waited until we had safely bought tickets to fly to Amman. We then embraced and said goodbye. I didn't know then if I would see him again. For all I knew, I would be living in Iraq from there on. At one level, I knew that, if it was the only way I could be with my kids, I would do it. I was so angry with Mahmoud, though, that to let him win in that way was unthinkable. My primary, overriding aim was to get the kids back, and take them out of Iraq and home to London, where we all belonged. I wasn't yet sure, though, which of those two outcomes was the more likely. And I didn't let myself think of any other outcomes. In my heart, I knew what we were doing was very dangerous. I didn't want to dwell on it or I might have wavered in my resolve.

The flight from Beirut to Amman takes just 45 minutes – they barely have enough time to bring food round before the plane starts its descent. They gave us some type of sandwich, which was hard and tasteless. Noticing that the kids hadn't touched theirs, one friendly stewardess went back to the galley and returned with bags of boiled sweets and chocolates, which Marlon and Khalid were delighted to receive. They settled back into their seats for the last few minutes, sucking on their newly received goodies and playing on their Game Boys, each with a burrowed frown and an intense look of concentration on his face. I smiled – that meant they were content.

When we arrived in Amman, it was early evening. The airport was bustling with people, as it always is. We walked through passport control, showed our visas and were waved through without any problems. Inwardly, I heaved a sigh of relief. I've always had a slightly bad feeling about Jordan because I was once deported from there when I was helping another mother. For that reason, I worried the authorities would have flagged my name because of what I do, so that whenever it came up on the system, an official would be told that I was *persona non grata*. Perhaps I was being overly paranoid. We were through, though, and that is what was important. We picked up our baggage, piled it on a trolley and went straight through Customs without any bother.

'Darlings, this is the important part now,' I said to the boys. 'We need to find a driver who's willing to take us into Iraq. I really need to concentrate so I want you to wait here with Auntie Tracey while Mummy sorts this out, then I'll be straight back.'

They both looked up at me with those dark, serious, almost mournful eyes, and nodded their assent. I thought my heart would burst, I was so proud of them. Here they were at Amman Airport, a long, long way from Maida Vale in west London, not batting an eyelid, taking the whole thing in their stride. Marlon was only just eleven years old, and Khalid – poor sickly, frail, brave Khalid – was not even eight. My babies. Soon we would all be reunited, I told myself.

I followed the signs for taxis and headed outside the terminal building. As anyone who travels regularly to hot countries knows, the first thing to hit you is the heat. It's like a wall of humidity after the false air conditioning in the terminal. I found the taxi rank and explained in my limited Arabic that I needed a driver who spoke English. For what we were planning to do, my Arabic would not be good enough. We couldn't afford to allow any potential misunderstandings. The stakes were too high.

The first driver I spoke to claimed that he spoke English, but within a matter of seconds it became apparent that his English was worse than my Arabic. A second driver approached who introduced himself as Mohammed. I said hello, and asked whether he spoke English. He replied that he did and had in fact lived in London for many years. That was good enough for me.

'Mohammed,' I said, 'what I need is a good, reliable driver who can take me into Iraq. I will pay very well for this, but it has to be someone who will not let me down. And it has to be tonight.' Mohammed seemed a little taken aback, but he nodded his understanding and said OK, he could do it.

I continued, 'You will need to stay with us until we are safely with that driver. In return for this, I will give you $200.'

He whistled. 'That is a lot of money. I will do this for you.'

I told him to wait there and went back inside the terminal building to collect Tracey and the kids. We came back outside and got into Mohammed's car and set off. As we drove, he asked us why we were going into Iraq. I told him that we needed to collect my children. I didn't explain that they had been abducted by their father. Mohammed seemed a nice man, but in the Middle East, sympathy is usually with the male. Even if someone privately thought that what Mahmoud had done was wrong, there was every chance that he would be reluctant to get involved with another man's personal business with his wife and family.

He drove for about an hour and we came to a small village. We pulled up outside what appeared to be a shop and went in. There were a few men there and Mohammed spoke to one of them, an older man with grey hair, dressed in the traditional *jalabiya*, the ankle-length tunic favoured by Muslim men. I noticed that all the men had oil stains on their hands and realised that they must have been mechanics. Mohammed spoke in Arabic to this older man for a few minutes, then he turned to us and said, 'These men can organise a car for you tonight. But the border does not open until 7 a.m.' – by now it must have been 9 p.m. 'You will have to go in the car to the border and sleep as well as you can in the car there while you queue.'

My heart sank at this. I had been hoping that we could get straight onto the highway that night and get some miles behind us. On top of everything, the boys – who had been so good and uncomplaining up until now – were very tired, and in need of a toilet and a wash. There was nothing I could do, so I hugged them and asked them to be brave for just a little longer.

After an hour, the driver arrived and spoke to Mohammed. His name was Alla, the same as my little boy whom I was so desperate to see. Was this a good sign? I liked him straight away. He came up and bowed his head, touching his hair as he did so as a mark of respect. Then he said hello to the boys – he spoke very good English – and set about putting them at their ease. Finally, he shared a cigarette with Tracey. Everyone was happy. We felt things were finally going our way.

I thanked Mohammed for finding this driver for us. He gave us his card and made us promise that if we needed anything else on our way back through Jordan – a place to stay, a lift somewhere – we would call him. I promised, and he touched his head and his eyes, wished us luck and left. I think he knew the real purpose of our journey by then.

We climbed into Alla's car after packing in our luggage. It was an enormous American car, long with plenty of seats and enormous wheels that meant you had to climb up to get into it. At least we would be comfortable. Tracey climbed up into the front with Alla, and I climbed into the back with the children. Alla had placed all the luggage along the sides of the car in the back and shut the curtains along all the windows. When I asked him why, he said, with a serious expression, 'When we cross into Iraq, there are bandits – I don't want to take any risks.' I realised that the luggage was placed there to try to stop any stray bullets. The seriousness of this final part of our mission was becoming clearer by the minute.

We swung out onto the road and soon we were on a highway heading towards the Iraqi border. The comforting rhythm of the car's motion combined with the warmth of the cabin soon conspired to allow me to doze off. Sleep was one commodity that had been in short supply over the previous weeks. After an hour or so, I was awoken by a strange noise that the car was making. I could see steam coming out of the engine. Alla cursed, pulled up and looked under the bonnet. He then made a call back to the garage from where we had set off. They told him that we would have to go back and change cars. My heart sank. It seemed as though, for every step we took forwards, we were having to take one back.

Still, there was no choice but to turn back. We arrived at the small workshop and got out to let the mechanics take a look at the car. It was amazing that men were there, able to look at the car, after two o'clock in the morning. It truly is another world in the Middle East. After an hour, they pronounced the car fixed and ready to continue on its journey. We all climbed back in and set off once more. We drove and drove. Before we reached the border, we came to an area where there were some shops that were open all night, one of those strange outposts you find near borders. Alla stopped the car and told us if we needed anything to eat and drink we should get it here, as there would be nothing on the Iraqi side. We went into one of the shops and bought a mountain of supplies to stow in the roof compartment – bottles of water, Coke and crisps for the kids, biscuits, bread . . .

We then drove through an area in the flat northern desert of Jordan called Umm al-Jimal, the Black Gem of the Desert. There are no lights on the road and hundreds of rocks scattered around on either side of it – a stark contrast to the flat desert we had been driving through, making it quite an eerie place. Mahmoud had once told me a story from the Koran which he said referred to this area. It was about the Prophet Lut and his indecent practices in the city of Sodom, which he believed was located in this area. In the end, Allah rains down a storm of stones on the city as a punishment to Lut for not listening to his orders, hence the landscape that exists today.

The same story is found in the Bible, where Lut is called Lot – and everyone knows the story of Sodom and Gomorrah. Seeing these huge rocks lying all around, I felt a shiver. I have heard other people say that the site where these stories from the Koran and the Bible took place is closer to the Dead Sea, near Jordan's border with Israel, but Mahmoud had always said that this is the area, and certainly the rocks seemed to support his story.

More pressingly, though, it is prime bandit and ambush country. I have heard many journalists who work in the region say they do not feel safe travelling in this area. Whether it's true or just a story journalists like to tell, I don't know. For our part, we managed to pass by without any mishaps and soon we could see the long line of cars waiting at the border up ahead. On the Jordanian side, there was a small outpost and the ubiquitous poster of King Hussein. We parked the car and waited for the border to open. On the Iraqi side, there were lots of American soldiers and tanks.

We took our place in the queue and nodded off for a little while. At around 6 a.m., the noise of bustle and movement woke me. Cars were starting their engines and pulling forward slightly, jostling to make sure they didn't miss their place in the queue. Finally, we reached the front and it was our turn. Alla handed over all our passports. The guard flicked through them, stamped them and handed them back, nodding for us to go through. We had got past the first big hurdle.

A five-minute drive took us to the Iraqi checkpoint, manned by

American soldiers. No one said anything. Would we get past them or would we now be turned back, all our efforts frustrated at the last minute? A young soldier peered in and, seeing a couple of Western women in the car, said, 'Good day to you. Are you guys press?'

I leaned forward and said, 'No, we're not press. My husband is Iraqi. He is in Baghdad with our children. We're going home to join them, now that the war is over.'

He nodded, as though taking the information in. Then he said, 'Could I take a look at your passport, please, Ma'am?' I handed it over and, as I did so, Khalid shyly held out some wine gums for the soldier. The soldier smiled at Khalid, took one, and ruffled his hair. He barely glanced at my passport, handed it back and said, 'OK, guys, go through, and y'all have a nice day now. Welcome to Iraq.' The way he pronounced it – *Eye-raq* – and the fact that this young soldier was welcoming us to this strange country, thousands of miles from his home in small-town America, only added to the surreal nature of the experience.

He waved us goodbye and we pulled off. When we got out of his sight, Tracey and I yelled with joy, laughing and trying to hug each other over the seats, saying, 'Yes! We've done it! We've made it into Iraq.'

Marlon, who is wise beyond his years, looked at us and, with his serious little elfin face, said in a worried voice, 'I think this is just the start, Mum.'

The sheer volume of traffic surprised me. It seemed everybody was on the road. Not far past the border, lots of cars were pulling over beside a fuel tanker, where the driver was transferring petrol directly from his lorry into people's cars. Presumably, the petrol stations on the road ahead had been closed because of the war, no doubt as the normal supply chains had been disrupted. It was strange to see so much traffic, so much disrupted humanity trying to get back to some semblance of normality. These were probably ordinary Iraqis, possibly from Baghdad, who had wisely fled the country while George Bush had been carrying out Operation Shock and Awe. For all the talk of precision bombing and pinpoint accuracy in their targeting, these ordinary Iraqis knew better – they knew that a bomb does not differentiate between the innocent and the guilty.

As we made our way along the highway, scenes of the devastation of war confronted us at every turn. There were huge bomb craters in the road, around which cars had to pick their way. Off to one side was a motorway bridge that had been destroyed and stood there angular, ugly and twisted, broken beyond any repair. The kids were dumbfounded, staring at all these scenes of carnage and destruction. I reassured them by saying that the region had always been like this, but kids are not stupid. They knew that this could not be right, and it can only have added to their discomfort. I kept telling them not to worry, that we would be fine, but it was as though I was trying to convince myself as much as them.

We had been driving for some hours on the Iraqi side when Alla said, in a grave tone of voice, 'You need to tell me the truth. What is the real reason we are here?' I told him the story from the beginning, leaving nothing out. He listened intently, without interrupting. When I had finished, he said nothing for a minute. I was very worried. If he had taken a dim view of what we were doing, if he had got angry with us for not having told him the truth from the outset, we were in big trouble. Without Alla, we could do nothing. I can't drive – and even if I had been able to, the sight of a Western woman at the wheel in a Muslim country would have drawn such attention to us that it would have made it impossible to get in and out.

To my relief, Alla smiled at me and said, 'Don't worry. I will help you get your children back.'

I felt a flood of relief. For the first time, I dared to believe that we were going to do it. My resolve had got us this far. With Alla's help (and Allah's help, of course), we were going to make it. I allowed myself to dream of being reunited with my children and all of us flying back home together. Tracey asked Alla if he was prepared to help us snatch the children if we had to, and he said that he was. I told him how grateful I was for all his help, and that he didn't need to worry about money; to trust me and I would look after him properly. I had a lot of money on me that I had begged, borrowed and cajoled, and if it had meant the difference between being successful or failing in our mission, I was prepared to throw thousands of dollars at the problem. When Alla realised that I had a lot of cash on me – I think it was the equivalent of around £13,000 – he suddenly became concerned and told us that we would have to hide it. He said that if bandits pulled us over, they would search our purses and bags, and take whatever cash and jewellery they could find. So we set about hiding it, putting bundles of cash into shoes, into the kids' trainers, down our bras, in our knickers – wherever we could find the smallest place, we hid cash. Eventually, we had hidden everything apart from a few hundred dollars which Alla advised us to keep with our passports. If bandits found that, with any luck they would believe it to be the sum of all our cash and leave us alone.

After that, he looked at me with a serious expression. 'Donya, I want you to take this.' My heart jumped into my mouth when I realised what it was: a handgun. He told me that there were three bullets in the chamber, though the safety catch was on. He gave me a quick demonstration of how to slip the safety catch off and fire it. I tried to say that I didn't want it, that I had never held a gun in my life, but he waved away my protests firmly and surely.

'Donya, I am not telling you that you will need to use this, or even that it is likely you will have to use it, but if the moment comes and you have no option, you will be glad of it. You are not doing this for yourself. You are doing this for your children.'

Reluctantly, I took the gun, wrapped it up in a strip of white cloth and slipped it into my handbag. Ironically, it was my best Louis Vuitton handbag. When I had bought it, I had been dreaming of glamorous occasions when I would get to use it; I had never expected it to be concealing a handgun as I went into a war zone to snatch my own children back.

A little while later, Tracey said she needed to go to the toilet, so Alla pulled over. The boys made the most of the stop by jumping out and having a wee at the side of the road too. Tracey didn't want anyone to see her, so she climbed down a ditch and disappeared up an embankment. Suddenly Marlon cried out, 'Mum, Mum, look!' I spun round, fearing the worst – bandits, perhaps? Who knew what? But Marlon cried out, 'Look, camels!'

I looked to where he was pointing and a group of camels were picking their way slowly and surely towards the point where Tracey had disappeared from view. They were chewing away, with a look of curiosity on their faces, wanting to see who this person was who had come to visit them. Next thing, there was an enormous shriek as Tracey became aware of these beasts standing beside her, looking down at her. She appeared in a flash, trying to run back towards us down the embankment, while attempting to hitch her trousers up at the same time. We were all in stitches at this sight and laughed as though it was the funniest thing we had ever seen. After all the stress and tension of the last few days, it was good to finally have something to laugh about.

Tracey didn't find it as funny as the rest of us. In fact, she was beginning to grow a little testy – she was exhausted. She also had a bad back, and spending hour upon hour sitting in a car and not getting proper rest in a bed was doing it no favours. I also think that she was growing more nervous as we drew ever closer to our destination. Towards early evening – we'd been travelling for 12 hours since the border and it felt like it had been days since we had last slept in a bed – we were coming upon Baghdad. Alla said that we had to change cars in the capital, because we couldn't take his car into Najaf. With its Jordanian number plates, we would stick out like a sore thumb in that holy city, so we needed to get a car with Iraqi number plates first.

Luckily, Alla had a brother living in a suburb of Baghdad. We went to his flat and all got into his car, his brother as well. Alla explained that it would be better if his brother came with us, as he knew the roads. With curfews in place, we needed to take the quickest routes possible. We didn't want to be out on the streets after curfew if it could be at all avoided.

We drove down to Najaf, which must have taken the best part of two hours. As we drove through the city, I was looking out of the window, trying to recognise anything that would lead me to Mahmoud's mother's house. It had been years since I had last been there, and, of course, it hadn't been a war zone during my previous visit. The streets were full of angry men wearing traditional dress, protesting against the Americans. It is a Shiite Muslim stronghold, and though they had hated the secular Saddam, who was from the north of the country, they seemed to hate the Americans even more. The streets looked unclean, as though no rubbish had been collected for weeks (which it hadn't) and there were tanks moving around. It was not a pleasant place to be.

Tracey and I got out of the car to see whether I could recognise something – anything – that would lead us to Mahmoud's mother's house. Tracey had no headscarf on and both of us were wearing trousers, which was a bit of a no-no. We should really have been wearing the full-length black chador, as do the women of Najaf. At least Tracey wasn't wearing a skirt, I thought to myself. All I could really remember was that the house was near a small hotel and a police station. By now, I was quite disorientated. Nothing looked remotely familiar. I stood there dithering, not knowing which way to turn. On previous trips, I had been driven there, and when you're a passenger, you don't pay that much attention to the route. We seemed to have come into the city by a different route to the one with which I was familiar. Furthermore, Najaf suddenly appeared to be far bigger than I had remembered it.

Suddenly, all the tension and stress we had been under seemed to get to Tracey, and she exploded. 'For Christ's sake, Donya,' she screamed at me. 'Can't you bloody remember where it is? Pull yourself together . . . I can't take much more of this.'

I stood there and felt like crying too. I was exhausted and felt physically and mentally drained. Tracey was right – I had to pull myself together. We had to find that house.

Alla called me over. He was very patient with me, not just because of the money that I was paying him, but because he was a kind, considerate man. 'It's OK, Donya, don't get upset. Describe this police station to us and we will see if we can find it.'

I told him that all I could remember was that it was on a corner, and that there was a small hotel nearby. He spoke in Arabic to his brother for a few moments, then said, 'OK, we think we know where it is. Jump in and we will go to see.'

Sure enough, when we got to the police station, I recognised where I was. I told Alla to drive up a residential street opposite, and then I thought I recognised the house. I jumped out and walked up to the gate, but then I realised it was the wrong house. It was very similar in style, with the same front gate. I could see that Tracey was thinking, 'Here we go again.'

We drove a little further up the street, then I called out, 'That's it!' We stopped the car and got out. It had an enormous black iron gate with a clasp at the top and a bolt at the bottom. It was open, so I walked straight in.

To my disappointment, I couldn't see any of the kids' toys or belongings in the big front garden. The front door was protected by a screen made of mesh to stop mosquitoes, and although this outer door was closed, the main door behind it was wide open. In the hall, I could see my daughter's slippers, so I knew they must be there. I pulled back the screen door and stepped into the hall. I could hear voices coming from the front room, so I walked in. Fatima, Mahmoud's mother, and her sister were sitting there and their mouths fell open in surprise. They started to get up and began to say something as a greeting, but I cut them off. 'Where are my children?' I asked.

'The kids are fine, Donya, they are safe, do not worry,' they said in Arabic. They came over and began to kiss me and greet me, but I brushed them away. I was feeling very emotional.

'I just need to see my children, you must tell me where they are. I have come a long way for them.'

They realised I was serious and tried to placate me, saying, 'They are with their father in Baghdad. They will be safe there. We will go to see them tomorrow, or maybe the next day.'

'No, we will go to see them today. I have not come from England to wait for another day.' At the back of my mind I also thought that, if they warned Mahmoud that I was here, what was to stop him moving the kids to somewhere I wouldn't be able to find?

'We need to see the children. I have Khalid and Hammoudi in the car.' (Marlon's Muslim name is Mohammed, but he is sometimes affectionately called Hammoudi for short.) 'They are exhausted,' I went on. 'We must see them today.'

Fatima came out to the car to see the children and then began to tell Tracey and me off for the way we were dressed. 'You cannot come to Najaf dressed like this, it is not right.'

I was getting tired of all this nonsense, and I snapped. 'I don't care how we are dressed. We're here to see my children, and I want you to tell me where they are right now.' She began to argue with me, saying, 'Mahmoud did what he had to do. You said you were going to divorce him. He was worried that you would take his children away, he had no choice.'

Right, I thought, that's it. I've had enough now. 'I have been pushed far enough now. I don't have time for any more of this. I am here for my children, these men have come with me to get them and I am deadly serious. You are going to get in that car and come back to Baghdad with us to show us where they are,' I ordered.

I will never know what I would have done if she had refused to come with us. Fortunately, I didn't have to find out; she obliged by squeezing into the back of the car. The vehicle we were using now was nothing like Alla's car – it was an ordinary saloon, so it was a terrible squash. We turned around and began to head back to Baghdad.

Mahmoud's mother seemed to be terrified. She was mumbling to herself, praying. At one point, I asked her whether the children missed me, and she told me that they didn't, that they were very happy. I think that was just a sign of how angry she was with me. I had never thought of her as a bad person, and I still don't believe she is.

'Why is it OK for you to be angry with me, but it's not OK for you to be angry with Mahmoud for kidnapping my children?' I asked her.

She replied that he hadn't kidnapped them, that he was their father.

'Yes, he is their father, but I'm their mother, and he had no right to do it.' I went on, 'I've been very good to your family, and I've been very good to you. Is this how I am repaid? I helped your daughter get into the UK and what thanks did I get for that? And as for your son being a good Muslim, don't make me laugh. He sits at home every evening drinking cans of beer until he falls asleep. Don't make me laugh, a good Muslim!' I was so angry now, the words were tumbling out of me. When I couldn't think of the Arabic word, Alla would translate it for me.

I demanded to know when I had ever put a foot wrong as a mother, when I had made a mistake, when my children had ever wanted for anything. Fatima couldn't answer me. She looked up to, indeed worshipped, her daughter Ibtihal, but I didn't see Ibtihal as such a great role model. I told Fatima as much, then said, 'Fatima, Mahmoud may not be a bad person, but what he has done is very bad to the point of being unforgivable. He has taken two very young children from their mother. They have not seen me for eight weeks. Is that a caring or responsible thing for any man to do?'

Poor Fatima was getting the ticking off of her life. She was not used to being harangued in this way, and she wasn't enjoying it one little bit. She leaned further forward and began to mumble her prayers again. 'The terrible thing is that you have aided and abetted him in all of this and still don't seem to understand what's so terribly wrong about what he's done,' I continued.

By this point, we had reached the outskirts of Baghdad. It was approaching well after 10 p.m. and Alla was extremely worried. The Americans had imposed a curfew of 11 p.m. and Alla did not want to run the risk of being pulled over. But I couldn't accept any more delays – we were so close, we had to see it through. Alla agreed to drive straight to the house where Mahmoud was staying. With any luck, we could do what we had to do without any fuss, then we could sleep at Alla's brother's house until the curfew was lifted in the morning.

In the darkness in the back of the car, I felt little Marlon's hand squeeze mine. 'We'll soon be seeing Allawi and Amira, Mum,' he whispered. 'But let's not be too angry with Baba. Let's just talk to him, please, Mummy?' The poor child was torn between his two parents (even though Mahmoud was not his biological father, Marlon still called him Baba and looked up to him as a father in every other way); he just wanted the whole family to be reunited, and for us all to go home and for things to be the same as they had been before all this had happened.

I smiled down at him. 'Of course, darling. No one is going to get angry with anyone.' But in my heart of hearts, I knew that things could never be the same again. Mahmoud had not only broken the law – he had broken my heart. And there was no way I would ever be able to put that behind me. There could be no going back.

As we drove through the streets of Baghdad, Fatima was having trouble remembering the way to the house. It turned out Mahmoud was staying with his friend Ali. I think she may have been play-acting because when I lost my patience and began to get annoyed with her, it was as though she suddenly remembered the gun in my handbag. Whatever the reason, her memory seemed to come back remarkably quickly and she leaned forward to tell Alla's brother where to turn.

We were driving along a main road beside the Tigris, the river that runs through Baghdad. Eventually, we turned into a residential street and drove a little way down it until Fatima said to stop. We had arrived at the house. Everyone got out of the car and I tried the gate. It was open, but there were no lights on in the house, and it was clear that there was nobody home. A neighbour came out of the house next door, recognised Fatima and explained that they had gone out in the car, but that they would be back before the curfew, which was now only a few minutes away. So we had no choice but to wait.

The neighbour offered us cold water, which was very welcome after the warm stuff we'd been drinking from bottles in the car. Fatima went to sit in the neighbour's garden with her, so it was quite clear to me that she had been to visit plenty of times, that these two women knew each other well. Now that I had time to stop for a minute, I had a look around at my surroundings. The street we were in was a pleasant residential street with houses on both sides. It was on a hill and below us we could see out over a lake, whose water appeared dark and mysterious in the night sky.

Tracey and the kids were stretching their legs. The lady next door came to her gate to chat to me. She asked me in English what I was doing. I told her in no uncertain terms.

'Fatima's son, Mahmoud, is my husband, and he has stolen my two youngest children, aged five and six. He planned it and, behind my back, abducted them. I'm here to take them home.' I asked her if she had seen Allawi and Amira.

She smiled and said, 'Yes, I see them playing in the garden often. They come to my garden to play with my little girl.'

I asked her how they were, and whether they appeared to be happy. She replied that they did, and added that she thought they were lovely children, very well brought up. I was happy to hear this; even with everything they had been through, it was clear they had kept their good natures. It gave me hope that they would not have been too damaged, too traumatised by their ordeal.

From the way she was talking, it was evident that Mahmoud had not told anyone what he had done, that he had tried to present it simply as a case of a father bringing his children home to meet the family and to stay with relatives. The hypocrisy of it all stank and enraged me. I even felt annoyed with this pleasant lady because I felt that she must have known what was going on, that she should have done something to stop it. Of course, it wasn't her fault at all, but when your children are taken from you like that, any mother would feel that there was a terrible conspiracy against her, that everyone is involved and united against her. I had seen it so often in the poor, helpless mothers I had aided over the years and now I was experiencing it for myself.

The neighbour was smiling at me, saying, 'Your children come soon with your husband. Then you all talk, there will be no problem.'

No one, it seemed, wanted any trouble. I heard the sound of a car coming towards us. As I looked around, I noticed that Tracey had disappeared. Before I had time to wonder where she might have got to, the car came to a stop outside the house. It was a small, white hatchback. Ali was driving. In the passenger seat was Mahmoud himself, looking like he had seen a ghost, and on his lap was my little angel Amira, with her cherubic round face and a tight head of ringlets. I remember thinking that her hair was much shorter than it had been the last time I had seen her, and that it looked as though it had been inexpertly cut. Such strange things that go through your head when you're in the middle of a crisis.

I yanked open the passenger door, but it was as though the rage had left me. Now I was calm and felt completely in control of the situation. Everything I had been doing for the previous eight weeks had led to this point and now that it was upon me, it was as though something greater than me was guiding my actions, that nothing could stop me now. I reached in and picked up my little girl Amira, pulling her away from my husband, Mahmoud. The look on his face was one of total shock. He had clearly not believed that I would track them down. Numb, he let me take her without any resistance. Then I pulled open the rear door, allowing little Allawi to jump out, his face lighting up as he called out, 'Mummy! Mummy!'

I pulled the two kids towards me, and stood there in front of the house, in war-torn Baghdad, thousands of miles from home. Khalid and Marlon moved closer to me and grabbed their little brother and sister, kissing and hugging them. Over the tops of their heads, I looked at Mahmoud and he held my gaze defiantly. I began to feel nervous for the first time. What would happen now? Who would make the first move? Was Mahmoud simply going to stand by while I took his children – our children – away, back to England, possibly for him never to see them again? Somehow, I didn't think so.

At that moment, as we all stood rooted to the spot, Tracey suddenly appeared, running up the road towards us. 'Don't worry, Donya,' she shouted across to me. 'I found a squad of American soldiers and explained the situation to them. They're going to take over now.'

At that, I became aware of a low, rumbling noise, the sound of machinery and gears grinding. I looked up the road to see two enormous tanks turning the corner and heading towards us. It was unbelievable, just like something out of a film. As they moved towards us, no one spoke. I suddenly decided to take control of the situation. Alla and his brother got out of the car. Mahmoud was instantly suspicious, demanding to know who these men were. I told him not to concern himself, that they were with me. Turning to my sister, I said, 'Tracey, take the children and put them in the car. It's time for me to have a few words with Mahmoud.'

Emboldened by the rapidly approaching tanks and secure in the knowledge that Mahmoud would not try anything in front of armed soldiers, I turned to him once more, moving with him into the garden – in spite of everything, I didn't want to let the children see their parents arguing. 'Mahmoud, how could you have done this to me?' I said, with a mixture of anger and reproach. Even now, after everything, I could not hate him. I could despise him for what he had done, but to me his actions were those of a desperate man, a weak man, rather than a cruel and powerful one. He looked so wretched and skinny standing there, like a little boy who knows he has done wrong and stands with a hangdog expression, trying not to snivel as he awaits the punishment he knows is surely coming.

He winced, as though to acknowledge that he had no defence, that what I was saying to him was fair and right – which, of course, it was. 'I loved you, I was a good wife to you, and above all I was a good mother to our children. And you took those children away. How could you? What have I ever done to deserve that?'

Mahmoud started to come out with some mealy-mouthed excuse. 'Donya, please, you must believe me, I was going to send for you. I thought we could all be happy here in Iraq . . .'

I cut him off; I was in no mood for his self-justifying cant. 'No, you were not going to send for me. How can you stand there and lie like that, even now, when the game is up? You wouldn't let me speak to them, you didn't answer your mobile phone, you didn't get any message to me that the kids were OK, that they were safe. Can you imagine the torture of having to watch the news every day, to learn that more civilians had been killed in bombing raids, and all the while never knowing if your children are among the dead?'

Fatima intervened at this point. 'I had no choice but to bring her here, she has a gun in her handbag.'

Mahmoud's eyes widened. I suppose he was shocked to think that I had come after him like this, with drivers and even a gun. To show I meant no physical harm, I put the bag down on a chair in the garden where we were standing.

At that moment, the two tanks finally pulled up outside the

house. There were several American soldiers standing on the tanks in full uniform with helmets, holding guns and looking at us. One of them jumped down. In the dark, it was hard to tell what age he was – he could have been anything from his early 20s to his mid-30s. I suppose he must have been in charge, as he seemed to be taking control of the situation.

He turned to me, and very respectfully said, 'Good evening, Ma'am. Are you the mother of these children?'

I replied that I was, but Mahmoud interjected to say, 'Yes, and I am the father.'

The soldier looked at him for a moment without saying anything, then turned back to me to say, 'Ma'am, could you come over here and talk to me on your own for a few moments?' Naturally, I did.

'You look after the children, Tracey,' I said, but he intervened.

'No, Ma'am. The children are going to stay right here with us until we've all had a chance to sort out exactly what is going on here.' With that, he and a couple of his men picked up the kids and lifted them onto perches on the sides of the tanks. Even in such a serious situation, the kids were smiling. It must be every kid's dream to be swung up by a soldier to sit on a tank. I could almost see Allawi and Khalid thinking, 'Wow! Wait till I tell the other kids at school!'

The soldier, who I assumed had a high rank, led me a few yards down the road, away from the tanks and from everyone else. He turned to me and said, 'I understand from your sister that these are your children, and that they have been abducted from the UK by this man, who is their father. Is that correct?'

Good old Tracey, I thought. 'Yes, that is correct, officer,' I replied respectfully.

'OK, Ma'am. Now, do you have papers or passports that will prove that these children are yours?' I showed him our passports, which I was carrying in a separate bag which I used to keep all our paperwork. He looked through them and seemed satisfied that all was in order. Then he said, 'Ma'am, I understand from your sister that your ex-husband took your children because he was angry that you were getting engaged to a US citizen. Is that correct?'

For a moment, I looked at him baffled. Ex-husband? Marrying a US citizen? Then the proverbial penny dropped. Crafty old Tracey had told these soldiers that Mahmoud and I were divorced, and on top of that, had obviously embellished my friendship with William – which, admittedly, Mahmoud had not been very happy about, and may have been a slight factor in his decision to take the children – up to the point that we were engaged to be married. Genius! No wonder these soldiers had been only too happy to help. Tracey had helped make Mahmoud the enemy – an Iraqi who had abducted his wife's children in anger at the idea that she could be marrying an American. This was to suggest that Mahmoud was some sort of fundamentalist, livid at the coalition's occupation of his country, not one of the cheering Iraqis who had welcomed the Americans as liberators. Thank God Tracey had come with us – that one little trick alone had made her absolutely indispensable.

I told him all about William – who he was, where he was from and how I had met him. The soldier listened intently as I spoke. I finished by saying, 'Now, all I want to do is take my children home, put this awful episode behind us and start to rebuild our lives.'

'OK, Ma'am, we can make that happen for you.'

I could have thrown my arms around him. People often criticise the Americans for their gung-ho attitude, but I had every reason to be thankful for their can-do, let's-make-this-thing-happen approach to problem-solving. It meant I was going to be able to turn around and take my children back where they belonged, away from this war zone – and nothing now, it seemed, could stand in my way. The finishing post was in sight.

We walked back to the others. Mahmoud had hold of Marlon and was saying to him, 'You and Khalid stay here with me tonight, and tomorrow we will meet up with Mummy and talk things through. Everything is going to be all right . . .'

I couldn't believe what I was hearing. Had Mahmoud lost his marbles? Had he become so detached from reality that he thought there was still a chance of salvaging something from this terrible situation – a situation, I'm sure I don't need to remind anyone, was entirely of his making? 'That is not going to happen, Mahmoud,' I said firmly. 'All of the children are coming with me tonight. We will call you tomorrow.' I had no intention of calling him the next day. If everything went to plan, within 24 hours we would be on a plane home from Beirut back to our ordinary lives in west London.

Mahmoud, however, did not let go of Marlon; he continued to hold him, begging him to stay that night. It was as though he knew that, if he let his children go now, he would never see them again. The soldier intervened, pointing his gun in Mahmoud's direction. He was very polite, but there was the unspoken threat that if Mahmoud did not do as he said, he would be forced to take action.

'You need to back off from the kid, now, Sir,' he said quietly.

'Why do I have to back off?' asked Mahmoud agitatedly. 'These are my children too.'

The soldier stayed calm. 'You need to back off now, Sir, because if you do not, I will be forced to arrest you. If you resist arrest, I will be forced to shoot you. Either way, it's going to make all of our lives a whole lot easier if you just do what I tell you and back off now. That's the way it works.'

Mahmoud realised that the soldier wasn't bluffing. 'OK, OK,' he said, letting go of Marlon and standing back as Tracey and I bundled all the children together, scooping the little ones up in our arms and shepherding them all into Alla's brother's car. Of all the children, Marlon began to cry at the sight of the man he considered to be his father pathetically standing there, being held at gunpoint by the American soldier. Mahmoud seemed to have shrunk in size and was stripped of all dignity. Once Marlon began to cry, of course, all the others joined in and soon we had a carload of wailing children. When these terrible ructions happen between parents, it inevitably damages the children, who want to believe that their mummy and daddy are the best in the world. They don't want to have to witness the dreadful fallout that happens when parents are at war. And this is why I knew I could never forgive Mahmoud. No loving parent would inflict this trauma and grief on innocent children who do not deserve to bear the brunt of one parent's anger towards the other. Even if he believed we were heading for divorce, he should have known that, just as I respect a mother's right to be with her children, I equally uphold a father's right. I would have never prevented Mahmoud from seeing his children. But, at the time, what he had done had put us beyond the point where we could come to a reasonable and adult arrangement.

As we began to pull away, the soldiers, satisfied that their work was done, climbed back into their tanks and, with a heavy rumble, began to drive off. As they did so, Mahmoud ran alongside our car, crying, pleading with us not to go. This only made the children cry even more. At that moment, I realised to my horror that I had left my handbag in the garden. 'We have to stop.'

Tracey looked at me as though I had taken leave of my senses. 'Are you mad?' she asked. 'We're not stopping for Mahmoud.'

'No, not for Mahmoud,' I yelled back. 'For my bag – I left it in the garden.'

'Oh, for Christ's sake,' she said. 'OK, I'll get the bloody bag.' And with that she jumped out of the car and sprinted back to the house, past a surprised Mahmoud, who must have been wondering what was going on. Fortunately, he was too taken aback to come and try to remonstrate with me any more. A second later, Tracey reappeared from the house with the handbag and doubled back towards us, past a bemused Mahmoud. She jumped in. 'Right,' she said. 'Now can we please get the fuck out of here?'

I couldn't help laughing. Even in that moment of crisis, I could rely on Tracey's no-nonsense, down-to-earth attitude.

Alla's brother put his foot down and we raced out of there. I was in the back with the children and I just kept kissing and hugging Allawi and Amira like you wouldn't believe. My precious babies were back with me. I almost had to keep pinching myself to check that it was true. But we weren't out of the woods yet. I know all too well from previous missions that the hardest part was not physically getting the children – it was getting out of the country and back home. For all I knew, Mahmoud could go to the police and claim that I had abducted his children. As I have said repeatedly, in a Muslim country, the father tends to be believed – and Mahmoud could cause plenty of trouble for us yet. My only hope was that, with the war, the police and courts would not be functioning as normal – and that they would have far bigger problems on their minds.

Back in the car, though, I kept cuddling the little ones, smelling them and kissing their heads, their hair, their faces. It was as though I wanted to immerse myself in them, to drink in every smell, every aspect of them. Amira was saying, 'Look at what Daddy has done to my hair, he cut it all off today.' It was true – her beautiful mass of ringlets had all but gone.

'Don't worry, my little darling,' I reassured her. 'You're still Mummy's little princess, and you're just as beautiful as ever.'

That seemed to cheer her up. Soon she was back to her cheerful, inquisitive self. She was sitting up in the car, looking all around her. 'Where's Dippy and Smudge?' she demanded to know. Dippy and Smudge are our two gorgeous cats.

'They couldn't come with us,' I told her, 'but we are going home tomorrow and then you'll see them.'

Allawi for his part seemed remarkably unscathed by his ordeal. He was gurgling away happily next to me, saying, 'Mummy, what are you doing here?' before switching tack to, 'Mummy, did you see those big tanks?' Everything was going to be all right, I told myself, comforted by the normal nature of their conversation. The kids would be able to put it all behind them.

Now that the adrenalin buzz of our adventure was wearing off, Tracey quietly began crying. I felt my own eyes fill with hot tears. The sheer exhaustion of the previous days and weeks was taking its toll. I strengthened my resolve and told myself it was not the time for tears – not yet. There was still work to be done before I could switch off.

Alla turned back to me and said, 'Donya, listen to me, we cannot do any more driving tonight. It is already past the curfew and we should not be on the streets even now. It is too dangerous. We will go to the flat of a friend of my brother where it will be safe for us to sleep for a few hours, but you will have to give him some small amount of money in return. I think it is worth it. In the morning, we will continue back to Jordan. For now, I think it is better that we all should try to rest for a few hours.'

That was fine – money was one thing of which I still had plenty. I asked Alla whether $50 would be sufficient and he nodded that it would be ample. I drew out a bill from my bag and handed it to him. A few minutes later, we arrived at a block of flats in what looked like a poorer suburb. We went into the flat and were greeted by the friend, who showed us to a bedroom where all of us could try to get some sleep. There were two beds, which we gave to the children. They were in such high spirits, so excited at being reunited. They kept hugging each other, and bouncing up and down on the beds as they excitedly exchanged stories about what they had been through. Alla and his brother came into the room and said they had to sleep on the floor with us, there was no other room in the flat. I think this only served to make the children even more excited. First, the tanks, and then their very own bodyguards!

Their friend checked that we had everything we wanted and

then slipped out of the flat. Alla explained that he was going to drive the car to another district, despite the curfew – it was better to be safe than sorry. If Mahmoud had noted the registration, it was possible that he might have come looking for us. Personally, I thought Mahmoud had been in no fit state to write down his own name, let alone the registration plate of another car, much less go out on the streets looking for it during a curfew after his recent experience at the wrong end of a US Army gun, but I said nothing. Better too much security than too little, after all.

Eventually, the kids quietened down and, one by one, sleep overcame them. Even I managed to nod off, though for how long I couldn't tell. At around 5 a.m., Alla stirred, got up and came over. 'OK, Donya,' he said quietly. 'It is time to get on the move again.' Tracey and I woke the children, who didn't look overjoyed at being recalled from the land of nod so prematurely. They sat rubbing their eyes for a few minutes, until their sense of adventure took over from their sleepiness. This game wasn't over yet.

I set to, giving each of them a quick shower and washing their hair. Amira kept stroking my hair and kissing me, talking nineteen to the dozen about everything she had been through, and asking when she was going back to school to see her friends. I had brought a lovely new red T-shirt from home for her, which she put on that morning. All of the kids looked impeccably turned out, I thought proudly when my work was done. We took a photograph of all of them there together, reunited in a stranger's flat in Baghdad. It would be good to have a souvenir of this precious moment.

We crept out of the flat and got into Alla's car, the one we had travelled in from Jordan. Inside, the kids immediately started bickering about who was going to sit where. Back to normality, I thought to myself with a smile. We drove on through the suburbs, on through industrial areas on the edge of the city, and soon we were on the open road, leaving Baghdad behind. Superstitiously, I kept glancing back out of the rear window, terrified that we would see someone in pursuit – Mahmoud and his friends, or even the police coming to take us in for questioning.

I told myself that Mahmoud would no doubt have believed that we would have left the night before, getting straight out of Baghdad and onto the highway, so that it would be too late for him to give pursuit. Besides, we had turned up at his brother's house in a borrowed car with Iraqi number plates. Alla had left his car with the Jordanian plates at his brother's house, so there was no way Mahmoud could now find us, nor work out which escape route we would be using to get out of the country. We could be going across the Syrian border, across the Jordanian one – indeed, for all he knew, we might be driving up north to cross at the border with south-east Turkey. And in all the years that I had known Mahmoud, he had not been the type to act spontaneously, to think on his feet. Even when he had taken the children, it had not been the impulsive act of a desperate man. It had been coldly calculated, planned over months. Even if he did decide to come after us, he would have had to go back to Najaf to get his passport from his mother's house, and he wouldn't have been able to do that until this morning because of the curfew. So I knew we had a big advantage, that we had several hours' head start on him. I felt safer for thinking about that, and settled back into my seat surrounded by my bickering, playful, adorable children.

I soon discovered one problem, though. While I was looking through Allawi and Amira's passports, I saw there were no entry stamps into Iraq. However Mahmoud had got them into the country, he hadn't done it through proper channels. He must have smuggled them across at some unguarded point. Typical of Mahmoud to present me with problems even after I had got the kids back, I reflected. An alert border guard would surely wonder why we were taking children out of Iraq when there was no paperwork to indicate that they had entered in the first place.

A few hours later, we reached the border with Jordan. Alla got out of the car and presented our passports to the guard. He flicked through them, looking in at us as he did so. Sure enough, it was just my luck to get one who took pride in doing his job thoroughly. He held out Allawi and Amira's passports and demanded to know why there were no stamps. Thinking on my feet, I explained that the two oldest ones had come with me from Jordan to meet up with the younger ones and their father for a holiday staying with his relatives. They had crossed the border through Syria and no one had asked them for visas. The guard accepted this, nodding cynically as if to say that he could well believe in the laxity of his counterparts down on the Syrian border.

'OK, no problem,' he said, closing the passports and handing them back to us. He waved us through, and we drove on.

As soon as we crossed the border, my mobile phone beeped to indicate we were back within range, that I had a signal. Alla phoned a friend to ring Amman Airport on our behalf to find out whether we could get a flight back to Beirut and from there home at last. The friend rang back a few minutes later to say that we had missed the afternoon flight, but that there was one in the evening that we could make comfortably.

Alla drove us straight to Amman Airport and we arrived with a couple of hours to go. Once we had unloaded the car, it was time to say goodbye. I gave Alla the money we had agreed on, plus some extra because he had been so good to us. 'Alla,' I told him. 'We will never forget you. Without you, none of this could have been possible. It is thanks to you that I have got my children back.' He smiled and said that it was a pleasure, and if we were ever in Jordan again, we must be sure to ring him and come to his house. We embraced and then he left us.

The feeling of walking out across the tarmac with my children to board a plane to Beirut, from where we could fly home, was indescribable. After so many false starts and dark moments, my dreams had come true. We were back together again, united as a family, and I would never allow us to be parted again.

Once we got to Beirut, it was too late for us to get a flight back to London. We would have to try to get one the next day. We joined the queue of people waiting to clear Immigration and to pay their entry fee to get into Beirut. Every time you visit Lebanon, you have to pay an entry fee, so you can imagine I'd spent a small fortune on landing fees over the previous weeks. I still had a knot of fear in my stomach. Even at the eleventh hour, something could go wrong. What if an over-zealous official queried the sheer volume of stamps in my passport? My to-ings and fro-ings would be hard to explain.

Fortunately, they simply glanced at our passports and nodded us through. We went straight to the taxi rank and asked to be taken to the Savoy Suites Hotel. I hadn't booked, but they naturally recognised me at reception. They smiled, and said we could even have the same apartment we'd used on previous trips. It was nice for Khalid and Marlon to have had that one tiny piece of continuity amongst all the random chaos they'd experienced.

We gave the children something to eat and had a cup of tea ourselves. I told the kids to play with each other while I made a few phone calls. I rang a variety of people back in the UK to tell them that I had the children and that we would all be coming home together the next day. Most people I spoke to were in tears at the news, as though they had never really believed that I was going to pull it off. Not with the war going on and everything being so dangerous and topsy-turvy in Iraq. How could they have doubted me, I joked to myself. I'm Jane Bond in a headscarf . . .

We put the kids to bed, all four of them in one big, king-size bed. They fell asleep, and I sat down and had a cup of tea with Tracey. We talked about what we had been through, re-living some of the moments of high drama, but managing to laugh about them as well. Tracey said she was exhausted and was going to turn in. I crept back into the room where the children were sleeping and left the door slightly ajar. From the light in the hall, I could see their cherubic faces as they lay sleeping. I pulled up a chair and, despite my fatigue, sat there watching them for what felt like hours. I was filled with love and pride, so much so that I thought I would burst. My babies, all back together again. It was the best feeling of my life.

The next morning, I went downstairs to a shop and bought some bread and cakes for breakfast. I then spoke to the manager of the hotel and explained that I had return tickets for me, Tracey, Marlon and Khalid, but I would also need tickets for Allawi and Amira. He said that it would not be a problem, that they had a travel agent that they used regularly who would able to sort out the arrangements for us, and he was as good as his word. Within a few minutes, he came to say that they had been able to get seats for us on a flight to London leaving the next morning. That meant we just had to pass the time for one more day until we would be going home again. I decided to do what every self-respecting woman who has been through an ordeal does – indulge in a little so-called 'retail therapy'. It was time to go shopping.

Beirut is a fantastic city, with lots of tall office buildings, as well as old architecture, all by the sea. It's a very modern city and has great shops. I went from one to another, buying lots of things for the children – new shoes and clothes – and I treated myself to a couple of new outfits. It just felt too good to be doing normal things with my children after all that we had undergone. They deserved it as well, and, to be honest, I felt I did too. After we had shopped till we dropped, as they say, we went round to see Lena, the fixer that Shine had arranged on our first trip. She was delighted to see us and was so excited to see little Allawi and Amira, safely back with their mother after all this time. Amira played with her little girls while we talked. Soon, it was time to go.

I decided that I would go back to the apartment with the bags of shopping, while good old Auntie Tracey volunteered to take the kids to the beach to play around and have some ice creams.

Naturally, the children jumped at the opportunity, and I left them walking off together with Tracey telling them not to run, and to stay close. Well, I thought with a smile, she'll have her work cut out for her now, especially with little Allawi! Now that I had them all back, everything felt so normal again. All the little things that you take for granted as a mother – the kids bickering, playing around, even being naughty – seemed so wonderful and innocent. I had never been happier.

Tracey didn't seem to be finding it so enthralling, though. When they arrived back, the kids whooping and clamouring, she rolled her eyes and said, 'Donya, they're driving me crazy already. I said I'd help you get them back. I didn't know looking after them as well was going to be part of the bargain.' I couldn't help laughing.

That afternoon, Whalid, our lovely driver, came round. He had sweets in his pocket for the kids. He told us he had a free afternoon and that he was taking us out for something to eat. Of course, the children shrieked with excitement and were racing to be the first to get in the car with him. I had forgotten just how noisy it gets when you've got all four kids on your hands.

Whalid took us to a lovely restaurant overlooking the water with a park just beside it. I realised how hungry I was. God alone knew when I had last had a proper meal. I ordered grilled fish with couscous and salad. It tasted divine. After we had eaten, the kids scampered across to the park, where I could keep an eye on them, and began to play, chasing each other around and shrieking with happiness and excitement. I felt a great sadness. They had been through so much – more than any child should ever have to go through – and yet there they were, playing like any normal children would. Children are so resilient – far more so than many adults, I often think – and seem to cope with some of the most terrible privations and hardships, bouncing back and being able to laugh and play. As I watched them, I knew that, however happy they seemed, and however happy I was to have them all back together, there was still something missing from this happy scene, and that was their father.

That is why I get so enraged with these fathers who take their children. It is so destructive. Once they have selfishly removed them from family life, it can never be undone. The love, the trust is broken forever. Even if I found a way of forgiving Mahmoud, it would never again be the way it was. How can you allow your children to go off for the day with their father if you are scared that he might try to do the same thing again? So, as well as the pain and anguish such fathers thoughtlessly, cruelly inflict on the mothers, there is also the question of what they are inflicting on a child. If they succeed in their cowardly, despicable plan, they are condemning the poor child to a life without his or her mother, and if they are caught, they will never be allowed to be a true parent to that child again, in case it happens once more. Whatever the outcome of their actions, things can never revert to the way they were – that child will have lost one parent or the other, either literally or in effect.

After lunch, Whalid took the boys off to get their hair cut. I went back to the apartment and made a few more phone calls. One was to Paul Hamann, the director from Shine who had worked on the documentary I had done with poor Alison Lalic. He told me that they were all so proud of me, and I was very touched by that. He asked how the children were, and I said they were all fine; that all we wanted to do now was get home. He was encouraging, pointing out that we would be home the next day; we didn't have long to wait.

The next morning, Whalid collected us and took us to the airport for what would be the last time. After we had unloaded our luggage, we hugged, and I thanked him for everything that he had done. There had been so many people who'd played their part in my story. I felt so grateful, and so humble, that they had all done everything in their power to help us, and Whalid really had been one of the goods guys. After extracting promises from us that we would be coming back to see 'Uncle' Whalid, he bade us farewell. Getting onto the plane for Heathrow was a great moment. It was really only at this point that I knew nothing could go wrong. We were homeward bound at last.

Chapter 13

Friends Reunited

When the cabin crew came around with the duty-free trolley, the children started clamouring for presents. Little Amira was asking me to buy her make-up – Chanel, if you don't mind, and she's only six! – and, although normally I would have told them to pack it in, I was only too happy to oblige on this occasion. I wanted things to be nice for them after their ordeal. One thing that I did notice was that Allawi had become naughtier since I had last seen him. Marlon and Khalid are sensitive, well-behaved boys, but Allawi is different – he's always been a little more boisterous than his brothers, but he seemed to be playing up more than usual. I could only imagine that his father had been spoiling him. A son is often more valuable in the Arabic world, and Allawi had always been the apple of his father's eye. Now, suddenly, he was back with Mum, and she was not quite as lenient as his father. He was too young to understand what was really going on. Like many kids, all he was worried about was how much he could get away with. At least he hasn't been too scarred by recent events, I thought with a smile.

We landed at Heathrow and, as we came through Customs, I was delighted to see Sharon Hendry of *The Sun*. I had called her from Beirut to pass on the news, but I hadn't expected her to make the effort to come down to the airport. She had a driver with her, and also a photographer on hand to get pictures. She wanted to get the story, of course. She was first and foremost a newspaper reporter, and she had to do her job, but I felt she and I had developed a bond over and above that of a working arrangement. Once we had taken a few pictures, we got into the car. Sharon said that the newspaper had arranged for us to stay in a hotel that night, away from all the media and hassle. Of course, all expenses would be paid for by the newspaper.

I thanked her for organising this, but told her that we would be going home. That is where the children belonged, and I wanted to start trying to get back to some semblance of normality. The children had already had enough disruption and excitement for one lifetime. Having national newspapers send cars for them to the airport and pay for them to stay in a swanky London hotel was not the way to go about bringing them back down to earth.

Soon we were back in familiar streets of Victorian terraces and double-parked cars. We were home. We all trooped up the stairs into our flat. The children immediately raced up to their rooms to check everything was in order, as small children do when they've been away for any length of time. Poor little Amira looked upset, her little face screwed up as she came back out onto the landing.

'What is it, darling?' I enquired gently, wondering whether this was the moment when the enormity of her ordeal would finally hit her.

'I can't find Dippy and Smudge,' she wailed plaintively. I couldn't help laughing. I explained that Dippy and Smudge had gone to stay with Auntie Ann, a friend of ours, while we were away, but that they would be back later.

Sharon and the photographer had come back with us to get some pictures. They had each bought the kids presents – Amira had a doll and Khalid some sort of football game. I knew they were doing their job, but it seemed like this story had touched these tough newspaper reporters in such a way that they were, above all, concerned about the welfare of the kids. They stayed until quite late that evening. I remember a flurry of activity that night. The doorbell never stopped ringing, as friends and neighbours dropped by, having heard the news. At one point, my phone rang and when I answered it, it was Mamoud, calling from Iraq.

'Hello, Donya,' he said, his voice faint down the line.

I couldn't believe his nerve, but I stayed very calm. 'Hello, Mahmoud,' I said lightly. 'How are you?'

'I'm fine,' he replied. 'How are the children?'

'Oh, the children?' I asked. 'Would you like to speak to them?'

'Yes, I would,' he said, his voice barely a whisper now.

'Oh,' I replied. 'Perhaps if you're a good boy, I'll let you speak to them.'

'Donya, please don't do this,' he said.

I was enjoying turning the tables in him and using his own words back at him. But underneath I am too soft to be cruel, so I went and got the children and let him talk to them. After they had finished, I took the phone back. 'Mahmoud,' I said, 'I'm letting you speak to them because I, of all people, know what it feels like not to be able to hear their voices. You can speak to your children any time you want, all you have to do is ring. I will never stop you speaking to your children because you are their father, and nothing will ever change that. Now, perhaps, you can think about what you put me through, and how painful it is not to be able to speak to your own children.' Mahmoud began to stammer out some sort of reply, but I flipped my mobile shut and cut him off.

Eventually, everyone left and we were on our own at last. I gave all the children a bath and got them into their nightclothes. We all sat on the sofa together, watching television, nodding off. The previous weeks had been tough. We all slept in the same room that night. I felt I needed the children around me, and, since then, some nights we still all sleep in the same room. We are much physically closer as a family now, with lots of cuddles. I've noticed that the children are like that with each other; they hug a lot, as if to reassure themselves that we are all still together.

The next day, Sharon came round to pick us up to take us off to a hotel in Hertfordshire, which is often used by the England football team, I believe. I had agreed an exclusive with *The Sun*, which had after all part-financed our expedition, so I was meeting my end of the bargain. As well as reporting that I had managed to get the kids back, which is why I'd had to phone Sharon with the news when I was in Beirut, *The Sun* was going to run a human-interest in-depth feature, so they wanted to go somewhere where we could do the interview without distraction. It wasn't too much to ask, after everything she had done for us, not just the money but the many extra little kindnesses she showed us. Besides, it was a day out for the kids . . .

That day, after we got home from the hotel in Hertfordshire, Andy Mountfield from the child-protection unit and his colleague, Margaret, came to visit us, as I mentioned earlier. I was concerned about some cuts I had seen on the soles of Allawi's feet, and Amira had a lot of insect bites, which I was sure were nothing, but it never hurts to check. The sanitation is very bad in Iraq, so to have a child walking around with open cuts on his feet and a little girl being bitten by insects could easily be a cause of disease.

There was one other thing I had noticed when I was giving Allawi a bath, and that was a big bruise on his back. I didn't really believe that Mahmoud was the sort of man who would mistreat his children, but, like any mother, I wanted my mind set at rest. Margaret sat with him and talked to him for a while about school and playing. These people are so skilled, they know just how to speak to children, how to get kids to open up, and it's by talking to them on their own level, not as an adult talking down to them. Then she asked about the bruise.

Allawi explained that he had fallen down some steps, and where he had landed on his back, the concrete step had cut him and left him with a bruise. We sent the kids upstairs to play and I talked to

Andy and Margaret. Their overriding concern, Andy explained, was for the welfare of the child. Having seen these slight injuries, they were not worried that the children had been in any way neglected or abused. Allawi's injuries were entirely consistent with his story, and he didn't avoid eye contact when he told us, or any of the doubtless many little tell-tale signs that experts know to look out for when interviewing children. Andy explained their concern was not that there was anything physical to watch out for, it was to what extent the children had been traumatised and affected psychologically by their experience. For that reason, he explained, he would like them to be seen by a social worker named Martha Chester. If Martha felt it was necessary, or useful, she would organise a social worker who specialised in these sorts of cases to be assigned to the kids.

A date was arranged for all the children to see Martha. She was very pretty and seemed very young, to my surprise – she looked no older than 25 – elegantly dressed and wearing make-up. She was very professional and we felt confident in her abilities. She spoke to me with all of the kids, then she spent a few minutes talking to each one on their own for a few minutes. Afterwards, she said that she felt the kids, although undoubtedly shaken up by their experience, were dealing with it well and were remarkably resilient, as so many children can be in the face of adversity. As for a social worker, she said that in her opinion I was coping very well on my own, and she didn't think that assigning a social worker would serve any purpose. I was glad for that vote of confidence. A lot of people have very negative views towards social workers and see them as interfering, or a waste of taxpayers' money – I'm sure there are situations where these criticisms are justified – but I'm not one of them. For me, I just think if you're going to help a mother with bringing up her kids, then you should at the very least be a mother yourself, and many of these social workers are not.

The reputation of social workers in London took a terrible dent following a tragic case concerning a poor little girl named Victoria

Climbié. She was a little girl from West Africa who had been sent to live in this country with an aunt. The tragedy was that her parents had scraped together the money for her fare in the desperate hope of giving her a better life and some hope for the future. But the aunt was a vile, sadistic woman. Together with her boyfriend, she took delight in inflicting sick and cruel punishments on this poor little girl, such as making her sleep in a bin liner in her own excrement and having to lie like that in an empty bath.

Victoria had been taken to hospital on occasions, and social services were aware of her, but nothing happened. She wasn't taken into care, she was left with that evil woman and her boyfriend, until she was discovered dead, her poor little body covered in cigarette burns. It was one of the most shocking and disturbing cases of child abuse in the UK in recent years.

Over the next few weeks, Mahmoud would ring regularly, full of self-pity, saying that he wanted to come home, but that he didn't have enough money to get back. It was unbelievable. First, he steals my children. Then, he won't let me speak to them. Finally, when I get them back, he wants me not only to feel sorry for him, but also to stump up his airfare home. Men make me laugh. They can be so cruel, so destructive, so selfish, but as soon as things don't go their way, they turn into whining, snivelling little boys who want Mummy to take care of them. Thank God there are women in this world, otherwise I really don't think anything would ever get done. I remember once seeing one of those silly stickers people put on their rear bumper, or in the back window of their car, which said, 'The best man for a job is . . . a woman.' Well, it might have been a joke, but as another saying goes, many a true word is spoken in jest . . .

But the sad truth of the matter was, like many other women in similar situations, I did begin to weaken and feel sorry for him. I know that I should have stayed tough and refused to feel anything for him, but people are not so clear-cut, not so black-and-white. I had always urged my mums not to feel sorry for the father once he had abducted the children, that they should do everything in their power to see the man put behind bars if possible. That usually didn't arise, because the father generally stayed in the Middle East; but if they ever did come back to the UK, I used to think they should have the book thrown at them. Now that I was in that situation I had so often judged from the outside, I was confused. All my old certainties had been swept away, and doubts had crept in.

One day, I got a phone call from Andy Mountfield. I immediately knew it was something serious from the tone of his voice. 'Donya,' he said. 'It's Mahmoud. He was arrested at Heathrow earlier today, trying to enter the UK on a flight from Amsterdam. He's being held at Paddington Green, pending child-abduction charges.'

Paddington Green? I was shocked. Paddington Green is London's most high-security police station. It is notorious for being the station to which the police automatically take suspected terrorists. Surely they didn't think Mahmoud was a terrorist? Was it because he had an Iraqi passport?

Andy reassured me there was nothing of significance in where they had taken him – that was where the child-protection unit happened to be based, so it was simply practical, as they would have people on hand to question him. Andy went on to tell me that Mahmoud would be charged that day and transferred on bail to prison, pending his trial. They would, of course, need me to press charges, he explained. I would naturally be their chief witness. I said that I would do it, but even as I said it, I could feel doubt creeping in. Yes, I was angry with Mahmoud – but did I really want to see my children's father locked up in prison? I had been told he was likely to get seven years – how would the children cope with going to see their father in the visitors' room of some horrible prison, perhaps separated from him by a screen? And how would it affect them knowing it was on their account that he was there?

I decided I would go to visit Mahmoud in prison before I made my mind up. He had been held at Wandsworth Prison in south London for about two weeks when I went to see him. The prison is one of those rather depressing, grey Victorian buildings that seem to rise up from the streets of terraced housing that surround them. On one side of the wall are people getting on with their lives – going to work, laughing, fighting, getting married, getting divorced – and on the other are desperate men whom society is punishing by locking them up. It somehow didn't seem right that Mahmoud was there, with murderers, thieves and rapists. He had done a bad thing, but it didn't seem right that he was in jail.

I was determined to show Mahmoud that he hadn't destroyed me with what he had done, that I was strong and in control. For that reason, I had made a real effort with my appearance. I was wearing a lovely Karen Millen trouser suit, although naturally I accessorised it with a headscarf – I am a Muslim, after all – and I had put on plenty of make-up. I was shown through a series of doors and gates until finally I reached the visitors' room. There was a counter down the middle of the room, with prisoners sitting on one side and their visitors on the other. And there was Mahmoud, in jeans and a white T-shirt like all the other prisoners. He was unshaven, with sunken eyes, and he looked a wreck.

I sat down. 'Hello, Mahmoud, how are you?' I was acting as though this was a perfectly normal situation and I wasn't going to pander to him or let him tell me how awful things were for him in this hellhole.

He looked at me imploringly, his hazel-green eyes beseeching me to show him some kindness. 'Please, Donya, you must get me out of here, I cannot take it, I will kill myself . . .'

I cut him off. 'Don't tell me what to do, Mahmoud. Before we talk about your situation, I've got a few questions of my own. First of all, I want to know why you did what you did, and then I want some detail about how you did it.' I wanted to get every last detail of his trip, like where he had changed the children out of their school uniforms. I already knew that it had been at Hamada's flat in Paddington, but I wanted to hear it all from the horse's mouth. One thing that he was able to tell me was that he had not been into an Internet café in Damascus, so either the private detective, Mark, had been lying or he needed to start thinking about getting better sources. Mahmoud was in prison now, so he had no reason to lie, especially not about something so trivial as whether or not he had used an Internet café. Then again, we're talking about a man who was able to kiss me goodbye and say 'See you later, darling' on the day he took my children, so who knows when someone's lying? The whole experience has made me far more cynical.

Sitting there on the prisoners' side of the visitors' room, Mahmoud looked pathetic. It was hard for me to maintain my rage with him. He looked as though he could barely manage to look after himself, to shave and be presentable, never mind mastermind an international conspiracy to abduct children and get away with it. I had brought him in some cake – as prisoners' wives and girlfriends do in all the best movies, only there was no file in this one – and a soft drink. I sat looking at him for a few minutes, not sure what to think. He kept looking downwards, too afraid or too ashamed to meet my gaze. Eventually, I said, 'You've brought this all on yourself, you know, Mahmoud.'

He clutched his hands and a look of anguish passed across his face. 'I know I have. Donya, please believe me when I say how sorry I am . . .' His words tailed off. There was really very little that he could say. When he had decided he was going to take Allawi and Amira back to Iraq and to his mother and family, I don't know what he thought would happen. Perhaps he really did believe somewhere in his deluded mind that I would follow him out there and that things would be all right. It had been the crazy act of a desperate man. I may have converted to Islam, but I would never be the sort of wife who would simply follow and obey. Maybe that was part of the problem.

One thing is for sure, though: he certainly never expected to end up in Wandsworth Prison on charges of child abduction, facing a possible seven-year sentence. That had put the fear of God into him. He tried to tell me that it would never happen again, that we could make a new start of it, but both he and I knew that would never work. I may have stopped hating him, but my heart had hardened against him, and, in truth, I now felt little more than contempt or, if that's too strong a word, pity for him. I still wanted some answers out of him, though, so I got him to admit that he had taken the children to Hamada's flat that morning back in March. I also told him that I knew he had contacted Leila, which he confessed to, adding the fact that he had even called her from Syria, which naturally irritated me.

One thing that I could not get out of him, though, was just where he had taken the children for the fortnight he was in hiding before he was able to get into Iraq. All the kids had been able to tell me was that it was up in the hills, that they had played in the street, there had been other children around and that Allawi had fallen and hurt himself. It wasn't much to go on, but Mahmoud refused to tell me.

'Listen to me, Mahmoud. You're in prison now, and it's over. You might as well be honest with me, because you haven't got anything to gain by lying now.'

He looked up at me, and he looked pained and sad. 'Donya, I am not holding this information back because I am scared of what will happen to me. It is because I am scared of what will happen to my friends. I do not want to drag them into this, and I know what you are like. You will go after them to punish them for their part, and I cannot let that happen.'

I had to admit that he had a point. But until I know every last detail of what happened, it will be hard for me to achieve what the psychologists call 'closure'. I want to be able to draw a line under everything, to put it behind me, and in order to do that, I feel I need to know every detail of what happened so I can make my peace with it. I had filled in answers to many of my questions. One thing that had puzzled me was how Mahmoud had found the money to do all this. His wages from the restaurant were modest and I could not for the life of me understand how he would have been able to finance the trip. Now I knew. He told me he had taken some of my jewellery and pawned it. I have got it all back now, thank God, but when I learned this it was like another kick in the stomach. I couldn't see how anyone could have stooped much lower. I had spent enough time with him. I stood up to leave, and Mahmoud said, 'Donya, please, you must help me, you cannot leave me here.'

I held my hand up to stop him, and simply said, 'No, Mahmoud.' With that, I turned and walked out, out into the daylight, into freedom. I needed to think about what I would do.

Over the next few days, I did a lot of soul-searching. I had always been of the opinion that these fathers deserved everything they got. With most of the mothers I had helped in the past, the fathers had fled back to the Middle East with the children, so it had been a case of going there undercover, like the Scarlet Pimpernel, to help to snatch the children back and take them home to the UK. Sometimes we succeeded, occasionally we failed, but the fathers always remained in the Middle East, so the question of what would happen to them did not arise. We were just glad to get back home safely. But if I had stopped to think about what should become of the fathers, I would have said that they deserved everything that was coming to them. I had always operated under the assumption the mother was the wronged party, that the father was bad. It had all seemed so black and white. Now I was learning that life was not so simple.

As I recounted earlier in this book, doubts about what I was doing, and the possibility that there might be more than one side to the story, had first begun to creep in when I went to Dubai with Sarra Fotheringham. I had ended up, if not exactly despising her, then certainly thinking less of her and questioning her motives, while her estranged partner had emerged with far more credit and honour than I had initially been prepared to grant him. Less than a year after that experience, I was learning what it really meant to have to analyse the many issues at stake, and to see that, in these cases of disrupted families, the whole thing can often be so much more complex than simply a question of good versus bad.

I looked at my own behaviour. Had I always been a good wife to Mahmoud? Had I always been the perfect mother to my children? I certainly do not for one second seek to condone or justify what Mahmoud did, but, in trying to understand it, I was learning that there are many sides to every story. All the media attention that I had been receiving, particularly after returning from Dubai – with newspapers, magazines and television shows ringing wanting to hear my story – may well have made him feel inadequate as a father and husband. He was struggling to eke out an existence as a waiter in a restaurant, while I was being given greater sums of money to appear on a television show than he might earn in a week. That can't have helped his pride or self-esteem. Arabic men are very proud, and can be quite old-fashioned, in that they feel it is their role to be the head of the household and the chief earner. Perhaps this is one reason that sometimes relationships between women brought up in the West and Arabic men struggle to survive – their expectations can be so wildly different. What an Arabic man would see as the right way for a wife to behave, to be deferential and respectful, a Western woman might see as sexist and controlling.

And then there was William. Although nothing had ever happened between us, it was hard for somebody from Mahmoud's background and upbringing to understand that a man and a woman can be just friends. My friendship with William would have been difficult for Mahmoud to deal with at the best of times, but coming as it did at a time when we had been going through a bad patch and had even discussed divorce, it might have been the straw that broke the camel's back.

And then there was the 'D' word itself: divorce. Islam allows divorce, but it is usually at the command of the husband. Many Muslim scholars say that if a man wishes to divorce his wife, he simply has to go to her and say, 'I divorce you' (some say that it should be said three times), and the divorce is effective. It certainly isn't generally instigated by the wife, though there have apparently been cases where Muslim women have applied to courts in the Middle East for a divorce. One thing is for sure, though; it's not usually the woman who brings up the subject. By hinting to Mahmoud I wanted a divorce, it was only adding to the, by now, long list of things that made me an undesirable wife and mother in his eyes. He was probably worrying about how it would look back home, and it certainly did not escape my notice that one of the first things that his mother said to me was that he had taken my children because I was going to divorce him. That would carry terrible shame and stigma in Iraq and, to an extent, even within our Muslim community in west London, where the people have had far greater exposure to Western liberal ways. In fact, one of the biggest insults a Muslim man can give another Muslim man is to tell him that he cannot control his wife.

I am not seeking to lessen his blame, or in any way make excuses for what he did. I just feel that I was in a whirlpool of confusion, where so many different thoughts and emotions were going through my mind. I could have done the easy thing, which would have been to go along with the prosecution, which would have made it all black-and-white: Mahmoud would have been found guilty, and I could have pretended to myself that it had been out of my hands. But then there was the question of the children. Did I really want their father to be locked away in some awful prison for seven years? How would I have felt, seeing their sad little faces as I tried to explain to them that what their dad had done had been a very bad thing and, as a result, he had to go to prison? They knew he had done wrong. Would it be right to punish them further by condemning them to visiting him wherever they put him? I knew in my heart of hearts that I could not do it.

Eventually, I decided I would drop charges or, more accurately, would not support the prosecution of Mahmoud as a witness. The decision as to whether or not to drop the charges would ultimately lie with the police, in the form of Andy Mountfield and the child-protection unit, and the Crown Prosecution Service. But, realistically, without my appearing in court as a witness, their case was scuppered. The problem for the prosecution would be that once Mahmoud's solicitors knew that I wasn't appearing, there would be nothing to stop them from saying that he had simply taken the children home to Iraq for a holiday to see his mother and relatives; that he was keen for them to know more about their Arabic blood and culture, as well as their Western one. Everyone would know that it was absolute rubbish – why on earth would anyone want to take their children to Iraq just as it was having the living daylights bombed out of it? – but they wouldn't be able to prove it. The case wouldn't even get to court. The prosecution would have to say that they had no evidence to offer, and the case would be thrown out.

I felt bad for Andy Mountfield and his team, who I knew had put a hell of a lot of time and energy into the case. It must be incredibly frustrating for police officers who work in the sphere of family-related crime dealing with child abduction and domestic violence. When they feel they have a watertight case, very often the wife or partner backs down, undoing all their good work and leaving the father free to walk out of prison. But I had always felt that Andy's chief concern had been for the welfare of my children, that their safety had been paramount. He wanted a result, of course he wanted a result – he was a policeman, after all – but I like to think that seeing the children back was, to some extent, sufficient for him in this case.

Before I went out to Iraq, he came to see me at home and I was a nervous wreck, unable to sleep, distraught, out of my mind with worry. The next time he came to the flat, the children were back, running around, and the place had been transformed from a depressing, unhappy, empty flat into a chaotic, noisy and love-filled place. I like to think that this was a result for him.

I wanted to explain to him that it had been such a hard, excruciating decision for me and I had not taken it lightly. It was for the sake of the children, who would have been distraught to see their father going to prison. I went down to Paddington Green police station with a bunch of flowers. This was something that I felt it was only right and proper to explain in person.

When I got there, though, the duty sergeant at the front desk explained that the unit had moved, I think down to Fulham in south-west London, so I never did get the opportunity to sit down with Andy and talk it through. I think he would have understood. At least, I hope he does now.

The abduction will always be a part of our lives. It is something that happened to us, and, in a way, it has changed us forever. It cannot be undone, the children will always know that two of them were abducted; it is such an enormous thing to have happened. The best way for us to deal with it as a family is to fully acknowledge it, to be quite open about the fact that it happened and to try to accept it so that we can all move on.

For this reason, on 25 March 2004, the first anniversary of Mahmoud taking the children and the beginning of our horrendous ordeal, I took the children out for the day. We went out for lunch, and in the afternoon we went to Queensway to go shopping. I felt that it was important for all of us that we learn to associate this day with good things as well as bad ones. In a way, we are endeavouring to see this date now not just as an anniversary of something terrible, but also something incredibly positive, insofar as it has pulled us together as a family and made our bonds with each other so much stronger. The whole experience made me look at myself as a mother, and look at what I was doing and how I related to the children, so some good has come out of it. By focusing on the positive side, I think it can become something that has helped us all to grow and develop.

I know from my own childhood and some of my unhappy experiences that you cannot sweep whatever is unpleasant under the carpet. Indeed, by seeking to do that, you give even greater importance to what has happened and it will only fester and grow in a child's mind. Children do not forget, so it would be an insult to their intelligence to pretend otherwise.

One sad thing about the whole experience is that I will never be able to fully relax now. Rationally, I don't expect Mahmoud ever to try the same thing again. But, of course, because of that dreadful feeling, that knot in my stomach when I realised the children had gone, I will never take them for granted. The children have now got mobile phones, and if they are ever a few minutes late, I'm straight on the phone. Mahmoud is not allowed to pick up the younger two from school without my prior permission. If ever I cannot pick them up myself, I have arranged with the school that a neighbour will collect them, a lovely woman called Umrakhia, who has children at the school herself, and understands the sensitivity of the situation. The school will only release the children to me or to her, unless I have instructed them otherwise.

Mahmoud has been stripped of just about all of his parental rights. The doctor, the dentist, any of these places, will only recognise me as the parent now. He cannot make or cancel appointments, and he cannot collect the children when they have to be there.

There was no way I was going to let him move back in with us and have his old life back, as though nothing had happened. He had given up his job in Maroush, the restaurant on the Edgware Road where he worked. To be honest, I don't suppose he really wanted to go and ask if he could have it back – not after the police had been in asking questions about him. Everyone there knew the story of how he had abducted his children, and it would have been pretty embarrassing for him. When he explained to me why he wasn't going back, I said, 'Not as embarrassing as it was for me to be married to a man who would kidnap my children.' But part of me did feel a tiny amount of sympathy for him. I pretend to be as hard as nails, but I'm very soft underneath, really.

He has taken a job as a delivery driver instead, and he is living in a guest house in St John's Wood, as he doesn't want to be too far from the children. It sounds like a depressing life, but really he only sleeps there. He comes around most days to hang out with the children, watch television with them or even play on the games console. I don't think it's his cup of tea, but the toys that kids have now, if you want to spend time with them, you have to learn to play their games. It's not all dollies and hopscotch, like it was for my generation.

So, he is still a very good father. He worships the children and is with them the whole time. I am keen for them not to feel deprived of a parent and, for that reason, try to ensure that their home life is as normal as possible, given everything that has happened. I don't want Mahmoud to be overly stigmatised for what he did. I will never forget it, and I would not let him take the children away, but I want things to be as normal as they can be apart from that. The kids have their phones, they know what to do if anything untoward happens. I do not believe that he would ever try anything silly again.

I recently decided that a positive step would be to move from the flat where we were living in Maida Vale. To me, it felt that it had too many associations with what had happened, that it held too many memories. Another factor was that it was right in the heart of a big Middle Eastern community, where everyone knew all about us and how Mahmoud had taken the children. I thought that it was time for us all to start trying to draw a line under the whole thing and allow the healing process to begin properly. For that reason, we decided to move and have taken a beautiful flat in Paddington. It is very central, close to Hyde Park and the West End. It is in one of these enormous terraces of Georgian townhouses that you find in central London, with high ceilings and great views. My only gripe is that it's on the sixth floor and there is no lift! My fondness for cakes and sweet things over the years has been catching up with me, so it is good exercise. As I said to the children, 'Look on the bright side, it's a lot cheaper than joining the gym.'

Mahmoud was a great help. He came round in the van he has for work and moved all our possessions. I joked that we looked like something out of *Only Fools and Horses*, with furniture piled up in the back and the kids squashing into the front with me. He looked at me and said, 'Donya, this time next year, we'll be millionaires.' It's a favourite line of mine from the show, and it's become a kind of running family joke, wheeled out whenever I despair of family finances or worry about things.

In spite of everything that's happened, in spite of all the pain, we're still able to have a joke and a laugh, and that's good for the sake of the children. A lot of their friends at school are being brought up in single-parent families, so the situation seems perfectly OK with them. He put up all our pictures and paintings on the wall, installed the kitchen, set up the television and did all the odd jobs that you need a man around the house for. The kids feel secure and loved with both parents around. It's about as normal a family situation as we can have, with our history.

Chapter 14

From the Mouths of Children

Eugene Costello, the journalist who has helped me to write this book, suggested that it might be a good idea for him to talk to the children about everything that happened and let them tell their stories in their own way. I thought this was an excellent idea, so, one by one, they chatted to him while I hovered in the background making tea. This is their story, in their own words.

Allawi, 5 years old
'I remember going away with Daddy. He said there was no school that day; he said school had finished. Then he said, Mummy's already in Iraq, let's go and see her. But she wasn't. We went to the airport. I said we can't go because Mummy's got our passports, but Daddy said he had them so we could go. In the back of the car, there were loads of things, like clothes. He had everything.

'Syria was fun. I made friends. My friend was called Mohammed. We played football. I saw a big beetle in the garden and Daddy stepped on it and killed it.

'When Mummy came and got us from Iraq, we went to

Lebanon and there was a Burger King right next to where we were staying.

'When the tanks came, I wanted to shoot a missile. It was great to see Mummy again. When we were in Syria, before Mummy came, Daddy hit me with a slipper on the bum, because I broke the bed. I remember crying because I wanted Mummy to be there.

'I thought I was in the garden and I said to Mummy, "Mum, can I have a drink?" And Mummy didn't say anything, and I woke up and I was in this other place where Daddy had taken us, and Mummy wasn't there so I started crying.'

Amira, 7 years old

'He [Mahmoud] took us to his friend's flat and we had to get changed out of our school clothes so no one would know what we were doing. When we left from the airport it was daytime, but when we got to the other end it was like it was night-time. We slept in Daddy's friend's house. I think he called him and said, "We're coming to your house." Well, I think he must have done, otherwise how could we have got in the house? When we went in the house, we were tired and we went to sleep.

'When we were in Lebanon, it was really cold and snowing. Daddy bought me some boots and a coat and a scarf. We went to a funfair one day and my friend, Ali, was with us. We went on a ride and it was really fast, it made me feel sick.

'I had a dream that Mummy came and got us. When she did come to Iraq, we got to the house and Mummy was there with Bibi, and Mummy had a gun. It was black, I think.

'I cried every night and wished Mummy was there. And when I wanted to ask Daddy something, I kept going, "Mum . . . er, I mean Dad", and he was a bit annoyed.

'Mum told me when we went, she was looking out of the window of the flat where we live the whole time and when she saw an aeroplane, she was thinking, are they on that flight?

'I think Khalid took my place with Mummy when I was away with Daddy because I used to sleep in the bed with [her] before we went away because I was only about six. Khalid was looking after Mummy when I was away and cuddling her. I slept in my own bed all by myself, and Daddy and Allawi slept in the other bed.

'When Mummy came, we were in the car and I could see this woman and I knew it was Mummy because I could recognise her nose. And she dragged me out of the car and we had a big cuddle. I said, "Mummy, Daddy cut my hair too short."

'And Mummy said, "Don't worry, it will grow longer soon, and you can look beautiful."

'Mummy chooses nice clothes for me all the time. I have nice things now because I'm back with my mum. Mum had come with all my Barbies, my toys, my clothes, she had everything. When I saw Khalid, I thought how nice he looked. And when I saw Marlon, I thought how big he had grown. It was all a big adventure, and I will never forget it, not in a million years. We went to a flat and we all had to sleep in this medium-sized bed. Me and Auntie Tracey slept at the bottom of the bed, and all the others slept in the rest of the bed.

'I still think Dad's nice, because he's still my dad. Whatever happens, I love my mum and my dad the same. I think Daddy was wrong to do what he did, I think he made a little bit of a mistake. He shouldn't have lied to us, he told both of us, "Mummy's in Syria, we can go to Syria and see Mummy now." At night-time, we were in a taxi and he said, "We're going to a house."

'We were jumping up and down, saying, "We want to see Mummy, we want to see Mummy."

'When we got back, the cats had got really big, because they used to be quite small.

'Now, if anything happens again, I'll scream and scream. If I get to the airport, I'll run up to someone in uniform and say, "Help, help, my daddy's taking me away and he's not supposed to. He's not meant to be taking me, he hasn't asked my mum." I'll kick him, and run away. But I don't think that that's going to happen. Not now.'

Khalid, 8 years old

'I remember it was a Tuesday when Dad took Allawi and Amira. I know it was a Tuesday because I have football practice after school on a Tuesday. No one picked me up after football and I sat there for about 15 minutes. Then Mum came and got me in a taxi, with Marlon. I didn't know what was going on. Mum came home. She told us Dad had taken Allawi and Amira. She was really upset and that made me upset.

'When we went out the first time, it was terrible. When we were on the plane, Monica bought me a teddy. I called it Brit, because it was a British Airways teddy, and also to remind me of Britain. I was always cuddling Mum and we were all crying. Now we are all back, I love cuddling my brother and my sister.

'On Mother's Day, I made a card for Mum and I gave it to her. We were in a café, I think in Syria. Mum seemed to get upset, but she was smiling as well.

'I remember Uncle Whalid in Lebanon. He had six daughters. He bought us dominoes. When we were going to Iraq, we were driving there, and I saw this bridge and it was all broken, like from bombs. I remember the American soldier saying to Daddy, "You have to give [Mummy] the kids, or I'll shoot you." There were two tanks. We were all a bit scared. When I saw Allawi and Amira, I gave them a big hug.

'After we got the children, we went to this man's flat. It was quite nice, and I beat him at draughts. Me and Allawi were trying to watch this DVD, but the electricity was a bit funny, it kept going off and on, off and on.

'If Dad tried to take me away now, I would run away and jump in a taxi and Mum will pay for it at the other end. If we were at the airport, when Dad was getting the tickets, I'd run off with Amira and Allawi and Marlon, and we would get a taxi or tell someone.

'I felt really, really sad when my brother and sister went. It made me feel isolated. When Dad took them away, I lost my way. But now I can pretend it never happened. I was a little cross with Daddy.

'I feel really happy now that they're back. It's a new life. I won't let it happen again.'

Marlon, 12 years old

'One day, after school, my dad didn't pick me up and I thought it was quite weird, as he always picks me up. It was raining outside. I went back into the school and I got the office to phone my mum to see what had happened. She said, "Right, wait there." She turned up in a taxi with William and we went to the primary school, which is about a five-minute walk. We went to get Khalid from his football practice.

'The other kids weren't at the school, so I thought, "Right, what's happened?" My mum was crying outside, so I knew something was wrong. I said, "What's the matter?"

'She said, "I'll tell you soon, I'll tell you soon."

'We went home. William was really supportive. Monica came as soon as possible, with Michelle, and we arranged the plan. Lots of people came to visit. Everyone came to see if we were all right. Because of my mum doing this for a living, I wasn't that worried at this stage, I thought we were going to get the children back. I was quite positive about everything. We went to Heathrow Airport about a week later, on the Tuesday. Usually, when we're in a car on the way to the airport, we're all happy because we're going on holiday. But this time we were all really quiet. There was an atmosphere that we needed to do well. We flew to Lebanon and we stayed in Beirut for a couple of nights in this really nice apartment, putting last-minute touches to our plan, what we were going to do.

'We drove quite a long way to the Lebanese border to get into Syria. We stayed in Syria, in a hotel in Damascus. I remember there was a sandwich shop opposite. We had nice sandwiches and juice. The first time we didn't fly, we drove, unlike the second time, when we flew to Jordan. It reminded me of driving to Spain, for some reason.

'When we didn't get the children, I was upset. I mean, any brother would be upset. But you've just got to put it behind you and look to the future and be positive. Never be negative in a bad situation. The second time, we did a sixteen-hour drive, we were driving for two days flat, apart from sleeping and eating. If you saw a picture of my brother, Khalid, he looked distraught, he looked crazy. His eyelids were down, almost closing. He managed to smile for the camera, but his mouth was smiling – his eyes weren't.

'We slept on the border of Iraq and Jordan for a few hours one night. When we were able to carry on, we got into Iraq. We decided to go to my grandma's house to see if they were there. When we got there, we saw their shoes on the floor, so we knew they'd been there. We looked around and we could see a games console there by the TV. Allawi loves playing on the games console, so we were sure they'd been there. My grandma was preparing dinner at the time. She said, "Yeah, they've been there, but Mahmoud told us you were coming as well."

'So Mum said, "No, he's taken them." She came straight away with us in the car to show us where he was. This was quite late at night, it felt really late because we'd been driving for so long. Maybe it was only about seven or eight o'clock, but it was dark outside.

'We went to the house in Baghdad. I was really tired so I tried to have a sleep in the back of the car, but I couldn't sleep properly, not until I knew where we were and what was going on. What happened next was, we were at the house in Baghdad and I saw my youngest brother. He came running up, because me and him are very close. I didn't see my sister at first, I just grabbed Allawi and hugged him, and it felt good. He felt so close it was like he was inside me. And then I saw my sister. She did the same thing, and so forth.

'Then I saw my dad. I gave him a hug as well. We looked at each other, but I didn't say anything to him. The next thing, he was refusing to give the children back. My Auntie Tracey was the hero of the whole thing, really. She called these American tanks. I mean, you couldn't really do anything better in that situation! She called them down, and they had a chat with us. My little brother was staring at them, and I was thinking, "Haven't you seen enough of these?!"

'Allawi got up onto the tank, just to keep him busy while we were talking to the other soldiers. Then we were all in the car together and we went to a friend's flat which we could use as a hideout because the curfew was on. We all played together and there were lots of hugs. The next day, we drove to Amman, and flew to Beirut.

'Beirut was like having a little holiday, and I think we'd earned it after everything we had been through! We had a couple of days to kill before we could fly back to London. Uncle Whalid took us to a restaurant just by the sea and it was really nice. I had grilled chicken. Most of the time, I didn't like the food out there so we ate in Burger King a lot! Luckily for us, it was just by the apartment where we were staying. When we were at the restaurant, Mum wasn't her usual self. She was quite nervous and didn't like to let us out of her sight. There was a playground by the restaurant, and Mum kept looking over and calling to us not to go away.

'Back in London, one day I came home from school and there was someone hiding behind the door. I didn't know who it was, but when I tried to shut the door, my dad jumped out. It was great. We had a really big hug, and he was crying. He said, "I'm really sorry,

I never meant to hurt you like this. I didn't know what I was doing, I must have been mad. I'll never do it again."

'I've forgiven my dad. I think he just made a mistake. Everyone can make a mistake, but you can't hold it against them for the rest of their life. I think even Mum has forgiven him, but she would never admit it. She's forgiven him, but she can't forget what happened. It's just really good that we're all back together, and Dad is round here all the time.

'When I grow up, I want to be a journalist. I want to travel and meet the people from the stories you see in the headlines. It's a good thing that we have moved flat. When Mum said we were moving, I was upset. But now we're here, I think it's better for all of us; it's a new beginning. It's easy for me to get to school. I get a number 36 bus up the Harrow Road, then I get a 328 and it drops me off practically at the school gate.

'I was getting into bad ways at the old place and hanging around with boys who were a bad influence. I didn't go straight home from school and I was just hanging around. Now I go straight home from school, get in, have a cup of tea and get on with my homework. If I am going to be a journalist, it's important to do well at school and go to university, so it's better to be here and not be distracted.

'I have already made a friend in a flat downstairs called Lawrence. He doesn't go to my school, but he's really nice. He supports Queens Park Rangers because that's the nearest team to here. I support Man United, but I like QPR as well, because a QPR scout saw Khalid playing football and said he might be able to get into their youth team. He hasn't rung yet, but you never know.

'Dad won't ever try to do anything silly again. He was just desperate, but he's learned his lesson. I think it was all a terrible shock for him. I think the biggest shock was having Allawi to look after for all that time. I love Allawi, but he's a real handful. That would put anyone off trying to do it again!'

Epilogue

Looking back, many things go through my mind, like when Sandra told me that Mahmoud said to her, 'If Donya is a good girl, she can talk to them.' I was beside myself at the time. I suppose what he was getting at was that, if I had been more like a typical Muslim wife, sitting at home, cooking and showing him lots of respect, that would have been being a good girl. But I don't really know what he meant by it.

I think his head had been filled with nonsense from sections of the community in Maida Vale; the men saying that they didn't approve of what I did, helping to get children back. As I explained earlier, the women all loved it, but the men didn't, they saw me as uppity. It's a small community, everyone is a neighbour, our kids all go to the same school . . . I think when I ended up in prison in Dubai, a lot of the men took the view that I was out of control, that Mahmoud wasn't in charge of me like he should have been, and that was probably getting to him. It was all getting to him. I was worried that he was going to have a mental breakdown. When the war started, that tipped him over the edge. It was on the news the whole time. He would be crying, saying, 'What are they doing to my beautiful country?' or going mad with anger at Blair and Bush. I really think he was beginning to go mad.

But it was worse for me when I found my kids had gone, so it's hard for me to be too sympathetic. There's a French saying, *Tout comprendre, c'est tout pardonner* – to understand all is to forgive all – but I don't agree with that. If I went through it all again, and thought rationally about it, I don't think I would have gone after my kids straight away, and looked for them in Beirut and Syria. I should have known what his plan was. I know him and how he thinks, so I should have seen what his plan was and where he was heading. And as events later proved, I was right.

In this book, I have tried to be as honest as I can about everything, to give a warts-and-all picture of myself. Some won't approve of what I have done, others will, but it's me. I hope some other mums will read about my experiences, and if it helps to stop even one child from being taken, to make a mum aware of the dangers signs, then it's been worthwhile.

Some, I know, will criticise me for not testifying against Mahmoud, but we can only do what feels right at the time. When I first went out after the kids, I was in a predicament. Should I be nice to Mahmoud in the hope that he'll hand the kids over without any trouble or should I be hard and take no nonsense? And then I realised I would do whatever it took. If it came to it, I was prepared to shoot him to get them back, that's how desperate I was. I was actually prepared to die for my children that day, if need be, and I had never imagined, even with all these women I'd helped over the years, that anyone would feel that way. My four kids were all there, my whole life was there, and I would do whatever it took to get them back. No one was going to stand between me and them. It was a big lesson to me.

It was as though I would veer between two personalities. I was saying to myself, 'How am I going to handle this?' A woman has to find her inner strength to handle a situation not of her making; she has to cut herself off from everything emotional and focus on the kids as though they are not her children. Like it is a job she has to carry out. That's what I always used to tell my mums, that these were not their children, to go in there as though they were helping a friend. Otherwise, it is overwhelming emotionally and they are not going to be able to do it.

So, once I had got them back, that anger had gone. It was enough that I had them back. Punishing Mahmoud would not help anyone, and it would deprive the kids of a father.

People have all kinds of different motives, but those were mine. With my mums, I always give them the benefit of the doubt – it's all about reuniting them with the kids – but that's not always the case. It quite often turns out that it's not just the kids, it's the whole family thing that they've been missing, that they have craved. They want the whole thing back, the man as well. But it can never be the same. I know that from my own personal experience now. Once the man has gone so far as to snatch the kids, all trust is broken, gone forever, and it can never be brought back. You panic all the time; you can't let him take the kids to school; you can't let him pick the kids up from school in case they run. It only takes an hour to get kids out of the country. People think it's really difficult, but think about it: if someone left my house with the kids, if I was cooking a meal or whatever, they could be at Heathrow Airport in 45 minutes. They could check in half an hour before the flight. So, in an hour and a quarter, they're in the air. Woof! They're gone, just like that. That is the reality of how I feel about Mahmoud now. I've forgiven him, but I can never forget, and nor can the kids. That's a sort of prison for him.

Two things in my life have happened that I'll never forget. Although I can't forget my experience in prison in Dubai, that's not one. The saddest things were when my daughter almost got meningitis and when Mahmoud took the children. That morning in Syria, on Mother's Day, when we were there looking for the children the first time, and Khalid came down to the restaurant and handed me a Mother's Day card that he had made himself. That was the worst feeling – I also hate Tuesdays, as that was the day Mahmoud took them. But I try to be positive now.

My friend Anne and her son were a big help when the children were taken, phoning around to see which phone networks operated in Syria to see whether we could bribe someone to release records that would show where Mahmoud was. We had been close friends since Marlon was about three, so over ten years. Her son recently died of cancer, aged thirty-four. He was very close to the children, especially Khalid. He wore caps to hide his hair loss after enduring chemotherapy, and gave a cap to little Khalid, who started wearing it. I saw him the day before he died and he seemed peaceful. I went back the day he died and he looked at rest. I kissed him and said goodbye. This was at the Hammersmith Hospital, a big old Victorian hospital down next to Wormwood Scrubs. It always seemed funny to me, having a prison next to a hospital. One's there to punish people, one is to protect people. And there are people in both, suffering different forms of life sentences.

Watching Anne's son die so young made me realise how lucky I am in life and that I should count my blessings. That's why I'm working on building up my relationship with the kids and – despite everything he's done – with their dad. He's still their father, after all. And I'm trying to develop my relationship with my mum. When I used to fight with her, I used to stop her from seeing the kids.

Mahmoud and my mum never got on, but now, funnily enough, they are OK with each other. It's as though she feels sorry for him after what he did; she knows what it's like to be judged harshly. I went and stayed at her flat with the kids for the first time in September 2004. We slept there. Maybe because I felt she deserved it; she deserved my company, she deserved quality time with the kids. And we have been back to stay there a number of times since. For the first time in my life, I don't feel she's being horrible to me, she's not making me feel bad. I'm the sort of person who won't forget and won't forgive if you upset me – I'll just keep away from you – but now I feel much more understanding of her.

That said, I'm very soft with my kids. When they're naughty, I'll shout at them, but they don't take me seriously. It's only when I'm really cross that they take notice, they can see I mean it. I don't agree with hitting or smacking, I've never done that. If you do that, you've lost control. It doesn't do any good. If you bring kids into this world, you have to understand they're little people, they've got feelings.

I think my oldest son, Marlon, had to grow up very quickly; all of a sudden he was the man of the house, having to comfort his mother every night. I remember after we got the children back, we were staying in the Savoy Suites in Beirut and Marlon was cuddling his little brother, and Khalid was cuddling his little sister, and they were all sleeping. Tracey had crashed out; she was absolutely knackered. I just sat there, watching them, with this warm glow inside. It was the most wonderful feeling. I wasn't out of the woods, I was still in the Middle East, but I somehow knew it was all going to be OK.

I smiled, and said to myself, 'It's going to be all right. No one takes my children.'

Acknowledgements

I would like to thank the following people:

First of all, my dear friends the Al-Jaff family, who gave me a lot of support when my children were taken. They lost their son to cancer last year; he was a very special man and loved a great deal.

My friends Sharon Hendry, Monica Garnsey, Paul Hamann, Michelle Ross, William Robinson, Lena, all the drivers, Latifa Rais, Andy Mountfield, Whalid Aslam and Martha Chester. I would also like to say a big thank you to Abeer Taher, who helped me out so much when my children were taken, and to my sister, Sandra, and her husband, Paul, for assisting me in every way they could.

Thanks also to the American soldiers who helped us – William, Deni and others. I hope one day I will be able to meet you and thank you in person. You are heroes.